Perestroika in Perspective

Perestroika in Perspective

THE DESIGN AND DILEMMAS
OF SOVIET REFORM

Padma Desai

PRINCETON UNIVERSITY PRESS

PRINCETON, NEW JERSEY

Published by Princeton University Press, 41 William Street
Princeton, New Jersey 08540

Library of Congress Cataloging-in-Publication Data

Desai, Padma.
  Perestroika in perspective.

  Bibliography: p.
  Includes index.
  1. Soviet Union—Economic policy—1986- .
  2. Soviet Union—Politics and government—1982- .
  I. Title.
  HC336.26.D47   1989   338.947   88-32477
  ISBN 0-691-04243-8
  ISBN 0-691-00386-6

This book has been composed in Linotron Palatino

Clothbound editions of Princeton University Press books are printed
on acid-free paper, and binding materials are chosen for strength
and durability. Paperbacks, although satisfactory for personal
collections, are not usually suitable for library rebinding

Printed in the United States of America by Princeton University Press,
Princeton, New Jersey

The author gratefully acknowledges permission to reprint an excerpt
from the poem "The Road Not Taken." Copyright 1916 by Holt,
Rinehart and Winston and renewed 1944 by Robert Frost. Reprinted
from *The Poetry of Robert Frost*, edited by Edward Connery Lathem,
by permission of Henry Holt and Company, Inc.

For Anurādhā,
duhitā divaha

Contents

Preface

IN WRITING this book, which is based on a lecture given in spring 1988 at Michigan State University, I have departed from the conventional treatment of *perestroika*. Instead I have taken a broader view that combines political, cultural, and economic elements. The political and cultural parts of the program are fundamental to Mikhail Gorbachev's overall design. Indeed, Gorbachev's wide-ranging reforms cannot be understood, let alone assessed, in narrowly economic terms.

I have necessarily confined myself to sketching in only the salient political and cultural aspects insofar as they bear on the major theme of perestroika. The core of my analysis is economic, reflecting my main expertise. I have, however, kept the analysis and style wholly accessible. Appendix 1 provides the necessary technical background for the arguments in chapter 5, which advances the thesis that the economic scope of perestroika to date is limited.

This book may be read along with the essay that introduces my recent collection of essays, *The Soviet Economy* (1987). There I analyze the several factors responsible for the Soviet economy's slowdown, stressing Gorbachev's need to make truly systemic changes. Since then perestroika and *glasnost'* have taken fuller, bolder, even tumultuous, shapes. The present volume is a logical consequence: the General Secretary certainly plans to keep not merely his fellow citizens but also Sovietologists in ferment.

In conclusion, I would like to thank Abram Bergson, Kenneth Gray, Franklyn Holzman, Holland Hunter, and Alec Nove for helpful comments on an early draft of this volume.

Perestroika in Perspective

Why Reforms?

IN THE final years of Brezhnev's leadership, the Soviet Union was by all accounts going downhill. The decay was visible on all fronts. While economists cited the declining growth rate of the economy (see fig. 1.1) as a surefire index of the malaise, others concentrated on recurring shortages, increasing corruption, and massive alienation. Moral and social values, an enduring concern in the Russian tradition, were widely held to be in jeopardy.

The declining growth rate was the result largely of the declining productivity of resources. More factories were built, but their output record was lackluster. The work force lacked the motivation to work hard and well. Besides, the growth of the labor force was slowing. Natural resources, coal and ores among them, were deteriorating in quality, and the best of them (in the wilderness of Siberia and beyond) were increasingly costly to extract. The drag on output growth could have been countered by the Schumpeterian drive to innovate. But except in the military and isolated industries, the Brezhnev-era record on innovative breakthroughs and new product and process technologies, and on their successful adoption, was scanty.

These problems persist. Perhaps in no other society, at a comparable level of per capita income, is the impact of an ongoing economic malaise so oppressive as in the Soviet Union. The pervasive shortages give a bizarre flavor to the daily life of the people. "The whole country is covered with blast furnaces," an exasperated friend told David Shipler (1983, 173) of the *New York Times*, "but I can't get a table knife."

FIG. 1.1. Soviet GNP Growth Rates: 1951–1980. Reprinted, by permission, from Padma Desai, *The Soviet Economy: Problems and Prospects* (Oxford: Basil Blackwell Ltd., 1987).

Elsewhere, the creative artist manages to capture the essence of the Soviet predicament in a few, luminous strokes, as in the following encounter from *The Master and Margarita* (Bulgakov 1967, 10):

"A glass of lemonade, please," said Berlioz.

"There isn't any," replied the woman in the kiosk. For some reason the request seemed to offend her.

"Got any beer?" inquired Bezdomny in a hoarse voice.

"Beer's being delivered later this evening," said the woman.

"Well what have you got?" asked Berlioz.

"Apricot juice, only it's warm," was the answer.

"All right, let's have some."

The apricot juice produced a rich yellow froth, making the air smell like a hairdresser's. After drinking it the two writers immediately began to hiccup.

More suggestive than the indifference of the saleswoman and the continuing thirst of the two customers is the pseu-

— Ну и дела! Целый день грузим, а вагон все еще пустой...

Рисунок Е. ВЕДЕРНИКОВА.

Fig. 1.2. The widespread pilfering resulting from the persistent shortages in the economy is illustrated in this 1986 *Krokodil* cartoon. One worker tells another: "The whole day we load, but the wagon is still empty." Among the items disappearing on the other side of the wagon atop the heads and shoulders of the quick-footed band of robbers are a piano, a rug, and TV sets. Reprinted, by permission, from *Krokodil*, no. 34 (December 1986).

donym Bezdomny, given by Bulgakov to the young poet Ivan Poniryov. It literally means the "one without a home." Perhaps in no other sphere is the wheeling and dealing, the endless scheming and the trading of favors (*blat*), more pervasive than in the citizen's search for an apartment in large cities.

Shortages breed alienation. There is not much point in working hard, in doing one's best, if one cannot spend the money on a color TV or a dishwasher. The Soviet social contract is aptly described as "They pretend to pay us and we pretend to work for them."

Shortages breed corruption, too. The have-nots must grease the palms of the haves. In the Soviet case, the "haves" are generally party members, who can procure almost anything in short supply—a Moscow apartment, an attractive job, a place for a child in a prestigious school or for a sick relative in a better hospital—but for a price. And there is nothing more alienating for the masses than the knowledge that those in power are corrupt. The legitimacy of the rulers, of the party in general, and above all of the socialist system, becomes suspect.

While the poor performance of the economy has created a pallid social fabric, political and cultural constraints have also played a role. Political participation of the Western variety does not exist. Literature and the arts, after a short thaw culminating in 1962 with the publication of Solzhenitsyn's *One Day in the Life of Ivan Denisovitch*, were forced back to the colorless world of ideological conformism and socialist realism. No wonder that foreign books and magazines are still among the most coveted items. Law and legal practice have continued to be restrictive of civil liberties. As for education, while Ivan can recite Pushkin and the multiplication tables, and excel in science and mathematics, the creative impulse and the incentive to translate ideas into concrete realities are lacking. All in all, the failures of the economic "base" are magnified by a restraining "superstructure."* As a result, life is so disheartening in the Soviet Union that it prompts the wry witticism: Religion comforts the masses by assuring them that there is life after death whereas communism does so by assuring them that there is death after life.

Yet there was a silver lining to the Brezhnev leadership in the decisive emergence of the Soviet Union as a superpower. But that status has proved to be a double-edged sword. For there is no denying that substantial amounts of the best resources are diverted from the civilian economy in order to maintain the superpower status. Continuing along that route will only exacerbate the current predicament.

Against this background, "Why reforms?" is a question that one can answer in various ways. "The Soviet Union will at this rate cease being a superpower" is the familiar response. "It could degenerate into a Third World country if technology and living standards continue deteriorating" is perhaps the economist's version. Gorbachev's answer, articulated appropriately to suit the time and place, takes a wider view. What is at stake, he believes, is the survival of socialism, a system that can be made to harness the productive forces of the economy to improve the welfare of the people. Economic arrangements must be changed with that end in view, as must certain features of the "superstructure." The external environment must also be altered, which brings the arms race and the conduct of foreign policy into Gorbachev's multifaceted agenda for *perestroika* (restructuring).

---

* "Superstructure" refers here and later in the analysis to the noneconomic features, among them politics, culture, law, and education. Politics includes not only the institutional features of the system but also the conduct of foreign policy, including arms control, regional conflicts, and human rights. I characterize reforms of the noneconomic elements in a somewhat eclectic fashion as reforms in the "superstructure."

The Legacy of the Economic Malaise

THE SOVIET economy is overplanned and overadministered. The special problems arising from this arrangement and the analysis of them have kept Soviet-area specialists busy for years. Indeed, if perestroika were really to succeed, it would take quite a bit of the wind out of our professional sails.

There is much that ails the Soviet economy, and the problems have been analyzed extensively. In assessing Mikhail Gorbachev's challenge and response, however, it is necessary to review briefly the salient failings of the system that he has inherited and that his reforms address.

Two events of momentous significance have left an enduring mark on the Soviet political and economic system: the October Revolution of 1917, which brought Lenin into power, and the industrialization drive that began under Stalin's leadership in 1928.

Lenin's hardheaded organization of the political life of the nascent state under the leadership and authority of a single Communist Party was matched by considerable pragmatism in guiding its economic evolution. During the crisis years of the civil war, the economy was organized along command lines under the system of War Communism (1918–1921). The available agricultural and industrial resources had to be mobilized and steered to the military. "The use of money was virtually eliminated, private trade was abolished, workers were militarized and paid virtually equal wages in kind, and farm output was requisitioned." The civil war was won but the economy had become a "besieged fortress." The peasants lacked incentives to produce and sell grain, and industry "operated essentially without direction, either from the market or from planners" (Gregory and Stuart 1981, 37–38).

Lenin's response to the economic chaos was to free the economy in 1921 from the heavy burden of War Communism by introducing the New Economic Policy (NEP), which combined elements of the market and socialism. As a result, the ownership of land stayed with the peasants whereas the "commanding heights" of the economy, among them heavy industry, transport, banking, and foreign trade, were kept under state ownership. But the management of industry, especially light industry, was freed from administrative controls, and private trade was restored. The NEP did provide the framework for an impressive recovery of the economy until 1928. But the economy was soon thereafter to be taken back in the direction of central planning and away from the market mechanism.

To understand the reasons for this, it is important to appreciate that increasingly, rapid growth rather than recovery became the pressing economic issue. It was therefore considered necessary to establish new factories in heavy industry that would provide the means for further growth of the economy. Workers in large numbers had to be drawn from the countryside for the purpose. The more rapid the process, the greater the need for adequate provision of "wage goods" (e.g., food) to sustain the industrial proletariat. In the historical experience of the West, industrialization had proceeded in a market environment; the peasant proprietors had responded to market signals to satisfy urban demands for grain by the workers and for materials by factories. While the process had not been altogether benign for all the participants—witness the descriptions of urban plight in the writing of Charles Dickens and of "bourgeois exploitation" in that of Marx—it had worked, on the whole, without serious imbalances: agriculture and industry had operated in tandem. By contrast, if the aim had been to push industrialization beyond this balance, with substantial investments in heavy industry—more steel and more machines aimed at more growth—then the market could not have been left to function on its own. The populace might have wanted to spend income on bread and shoes, but if the priority of the state had been to build steel mills, the populace and the market would have had to yield to the state and its objectives. Administered allocations would then have been a necessary policy requirement, a natural consequence of the state's objectives.

The Soviet First Five-Year Plan launched under Stalin in 1928 embodied precisely such a vision of rapid industrialization and, therefore, the need for administered direction. (The basic features of the planned system that Gorbachev inherited nearly six decades later were laid out then.) Industry, which was largely under state ownership, began to be administered by production targets and materials allocations. There had to be a plan, and bureaucrats to supervise and enforce its implementation. There was also the problem of extracting surplus grain from the peasants (who still owned the land), so that the urban population, increasing by leaps and bounds, could be fed. In a market system, the peasants would be offered attractive prices. But Stalin's answer in 1929 was collectivization and abolition of independent farms. The peasants on the collective farms would not be left free to decide how much to produce and what amount to sell to the state. Even the free choice of occupations by workers was suspended during the 1930s when factories were outbidding each other in their search for skilled manpower. While freedom of occupation was restored after World War II, the remaining features of the Stalinist overplanned and overadministered system were more or less intact when Gorbachev rose to leadership.

INDUSTRY

Soviet industrial enterprises operate within the framework of a production-financial-technological plan assigned to them by state planners. The bonus earned by the workers and managers depends on the fulfillment of this plan. The bonus is over and above the earnings based on payment scales set by the planners and distinguished by type of skill, the nature of the work, and the location of the factories. The workers in Siberia, for example, are paid at a higher rate than similar workers elsewhere.

The main elements of the production plan are the output targets, the allocation of the required inputs, and a wage bill. What are the criteria, or rules, in terms of which planners decide that enterprise managers have fulfilled the plan assigned to them? The story here is that of a continuing hunt by the planners for the best rules.

It began with the infamous gross output (*val*) targets: so many tons to be produced, so many acres to be tilled, so many pages or books to be printed, so many patients per day to be examined by a doctor, and so on. The managers have kept ahead of the planners, and the cartoonists have had a field day. A particularly telling cartoon in *Krokodil* depicts a factory manager who has produced a single gigantic nail in fulfillment of a target specified in tons rather than as an assortment of nails. And why would anyone want to plough the fields adequately if the mere number of acres ploughed was the only target to meet? Alec Nove's (1977, 139) favorite story is of the farm apparatchik who tells the tractor operator to "plough deeper" because the inspector is visible on the horizon. Successfully meeting the target for books can be managed by changing the size of the page or the print, or, in desperation, the margins. Naturally enough, val targets do not encourage a concern for saving materials, labor productivity, or for product quality.

It was not until the Kosygin reforms of 1965 that sales revenue and profits appeared as additional criteria. What was produced was now to be sold so that inventories would not accumulate. And profits, hitherto barred as a bourgeois contamination, could help raise productivity and save materials. However, managerial bonuses (while related to profits) are still contingent on the fulfillment of the gross output target. Like Jaws in James Bond films, val cannot be vanquished. General Secretary Gorbachev referred to it in his speech at the Party Conference in June 1988, somewhat in exasperation: "Oh, how many faithful followers we have of 'gross output!' " (*Pravda*, June 29,

1988). How can it be otherwise? The national plan is mandated and worked out in terms of physical targets; clearly, the plan would fall apart if these are not met. So val continues to dominate, while rules aimed at mitigating its outrageous consequences have proliferated.

The overall wage bill is specified by the planners and cannot be exceeded. It is hoped that labor productivity will then keep ahead of wage payments. That is more easily said than done because, while managers can shuffle workers around, there are legal restrictions and trade union pressures against dismissals. Nor are managers keen to cut down on the use of materials, because they are under pressure to fulfill val rather than make profits. Therefore, in the 1965 reforms, economy of materials use was sought through setting upper limits on their use. In practice, however, given the shortages and unreliable supplies from the state agency, managers tend to hoard materials and spare parts. When their stocks dry up, these same managers can count on the *tolkachi*, the special breed of Soviet middlemen, to cut through the bureaucratic red tape and procure the item, if necessary, from illegal sources.

The production plan has a matching financial plan. Revenues, costs, and profits are calculated in terms of prices set by the State Price Committee. The price, so-called, is the average cost of a product plus a normal profit rate. When these official prices deviate from prevailing average costs, prices are revised. So far, this ritual is the essence of the successive Soviet price reforms. But the Price Committee cannot cope with the task of fixing prices of the new items that appear every now and then. Therefore, enterprise managers can legally charge higher prices on new products of better quality. And they certainly do, because higher prices, given the gross output targets, add to sales revenues, profits, and bonuses.

A technical, cost-accounting detail of the financial plan is the budgetary system of *khozraschet* whereby enterprises are expected to finance their operating expenses out of their sales revenue. In actual practice, however, if receipts exceed expenditures, a portion of the profits is handed over to the state budget, whereas if receipts fall short of expenses, the enterprise gets a subsidy from the state budget. Bankruptcies are not permitted in this "squatters' rights" paradise; Soviet enterprises do not go out of business because they have losses. This seems like an advantageous situation for Soviet workers, but, in fact, the persistence of the resulting inefficiencies damages the performance of the whole economy and ultimately hurts the workers as well.

The most damaging feature of the arrangement is the technical plan for an enterprise that sets out targets for technological innovation in products and processes. The planners have sought to promote innovation via command rather than demand. If a proposal for a new item or process is approved, it is incorporated in the enterprise plan. Such a proposal may originate from the R & D laboratory of the enterprise or may be suggested by the design bureau of the relevant ministry. Once the proposal is included in the plan, the enterprise is responsible for carrying it out. The enterprise planning, design, and technological departments collaborate on the choice of the production technique and the required changes in the plant layout for producing the new output. Could Steve Wozniak have invented the microcomputer in such a system?

And how are these activities financed? The money is allocated by the ministries from the "unified fund for the development of science and technology" (*edinii fond razvitiia nauki i tekhniki*). This fund is financed from levies on enterprises and associations that are deposited in accounts with the ministries. It would seem that what "big brother" gives with one hand, he takes with another. After an innovation has been developed, production using finances from the fund cannot begin without prior approval of the appropriate ministry. Other negative aspects abound. There is an enormous amount of paperwork, from the initial application for funding to the periodic progress reports to the final project fulfillment report. The amount of the levy is not related to the performance of the innovating enterprise. It is possible that the project will be completed on schedule, and it may even turn out to be a first-rate item. However, there are no rewards for that. The successful innovator's relative contribution to the ministerial fund is about the same as that of a tardy, less skilled performer. It may even be bigger.

Outside of this plan, there is one other way for a daring group to produce a new product or initiate a new process. An enterprise can team up with another unit for R & D and production. The enterprise can finance this activity from funds at its disposal from its profits. But the drag on being a Schumpeterian trailblazer comes from the dominance of the output rule in judging performance. New products tend to lower current production because machines must be retooled and labor must be retrained. "The decline in [current] output is rarely compensated by the higher price of the new product" (U.S. Department of Commerce 1985, 45). A Soviet manager would prefer to stay on the well-trodden shore rather than sail out in uncharted waters.

And these are indeed uncharted waters because of the further problem of marketing the new products. They are allotted by the State Committee on Supply to various allocation centers (*fondoderzhateli*) for distribution to sales organizations or a customer enterprise. The enterprise is thus left at the mercy of another agency and its "efficient administration work" for fulfilling its sales target (Berliner 1976, 210). But "administrative efficiency" can hardly resolve the problem of mismatched supply and demand, especially when new products are at stake.

Soviet innovative activity is thus not only devoid of the what's-in-it-for-me motivation found in a competitive environment but the decision making involved, from R & D to market sales, is fragmented.

No wonder then that the record of technological innovation and performance is sluggish and haphazard. In defense production, the Soviet achievements are, of course, sustained and impressive. Whereas U.S. leads in the major underlying technologies are generally believed to outnumber U.S. lags, "ingenious and effective Soviet design frequently generates . . . weapons systems that are comparable in effectiveness with those of the US" (Hanson 1981, 41–42). In electricity generation, transmission, and supply, Soviet performance is also strong. It began back in the early twenties when Lenin identified communism with *elektrifikatsiia* and soviet power. In other high-priority industries such as iron, steel, and machine tools, the achievements consist in updating current technologies and widespread production of items such as large open-hearth furnaces and standard machine tools. But in the area of more sophisticated products, such as oxygen convertors and electric steel and automated machine tools, the record is patchy: there are delays in diffusion, the product mix is highly standardized, and the quality not always reliable. Abel Aganbegyan (1988, 96) laments over the fact that although the continuous casting of steel was pioneered by the Soviets, the Japanese have forged ahead in its application. Overall, there is a decisive lag in high tech (in computers, electronics, and chemicals) and in a wide array of consumer goods (in processed foods, sophisticated durables, fancy textiles, and footwear). While Soviet satellites orbit the earth and perform outstanding feats, the industrial landscape below has remained untouched by the telecommunications and electronics revolutions. Gorbachev wants to retire the dinosaurs in industry and bring in the new breed of versatile performers. He wants to transform people's lives by introducing variety, quality, and color. The renovation of industry and the enrichment of consumption will require giant strides in new technologies and their diffusion; performance so far in these areas is inadequate to meet the challenges.

AGRICULTURE

The problems of Soviet agriculture are more serious. While a few superstar industries may be credited with catapulting the Soviet Union into a superpower, agriculture's lagging performance makes a massive dent in that image. Many ask why a superpower has needed to import up to forty million tons of grain a year recently.

First, a few facts to set the record straight. Soviet yields of winter wheat in the Ukraine, for example, are quite respectable. Until recently, grain yields had been rising for a little over two decades. Nor is there any malnourishment, reminiscent of the Third World, in the Soviet Union.

What, then, is wrong? Weather undoubtedly plays a negative role. Because of the extreme, northern location of the Soviet grain belt, winters are long and severe, and the growing season is very short. The moisture diminishes as one travels southeast toward the dry regions of central Asia and Kazakhstan. Given the inhospitable climate and large tracts of unfavorable soil in the arable lands, the central questions have been: How should farming be organized? Where should it be concentrated? With Stalin's collectivization in the early 1930s, socialist agriculture, with the division of farms into collective and state units, became an additional albatross for the Soviet countryside. All devices to wrestle with the weather and low soil productivity had to be adopted within the framework of this Procrustean socialist bed. Stalin responded to the challenge with mechanization, Khrushchev extended farming into the Virgin Lands, and Brezhnev poured massive resources into agriculture and agro-industrial complexes. With rising procurement prices (beginning around 1967) on most agricultural produce and with fixed prices paid by consumers for food items, the payment of agricultural subsidies from the state budget has gone out of control.

Despite the investments, the perennial problems of Soviet agriculture persist: lack of roads, machines largely out of order, fertilizers in the wrong mix with no machines to spread them, and inadequate storage on farms and elsewhere. Grain wasted each year roughly equals grain imported in recent years. The consumers, for their part, apparently continue to cope stoically with the same problems: the recurring meat shortages; the legendary lines for lemons in Moscow winters; and the usual diet of kvasha, kolbasa, carrots, and cabbages, with culinary delights out of reach for all but a few. The Soviet Union actually produces more milk and butter than the United States, but fewer than a dozen different cheeses are available in Moscow stores.

Agriculture exhibits the same array of symptoms as industry: inefficiency, waste, and lack of product variety. The underlying causes are similar, arising from the absence of farm-level freedom, incentives, and response to market demands.

The output targets for grains, cash crops, and livestock products are handed down by central planners. From the midsixties, they have been set for five years, providing the farms with a stable set of tasks. The product mix can be varied, but only within limits. The materials are similarly allotted. The plowing, sowing, and harvesting by the farm households proceed with helpful hints from the farm managers, occasional tips, mostly unwelcome, from the local party operatives, and all-too-frequent proddings from the ministerial watchdogs.

As for incentives, they appeared on Soviet farms somewhat late, toward the end of the Brezhnev years when the contract system was introduced. It was intended to promote incentives and encourage better performance. But what was wrong with the old arrangement?

In the traditional setting, the farm, which exceeds two thousand acres on average, is the unit of cultivation and management. The workers on state farms (*sovkhozy*) are guaranteed a fixed wage as in factories, whereas on collective farms (*kolkhozy*) they can earn a bonus if output targets are exceeded. The chores of tilling, planting, and harvesting in both cases are handed out to households by the farm management. But the farms are huge, the work force is large, and continuous supervision is necessary to wrestle with the "free rider" problem. Everyone wants a bountiful harvest while hoping that the next fellow will do his best.

In the new, contract arrangement, the collective farm is divided into plots that are handed over to groups of farm families. They sign a contract with the farm management for delivering specified amounts of crops or livestock for which, again, they are allotted machines and materials. They earn a bonus if they produce more than what they have promised. The families may be combined in a link (*zveno*), which is smaller than the alternative arrangement of a brigade (*brigada*). They carry out the entire sequence from plowing to harvesting, and their bonus depends on how well they manage their piece of land. The connection between effort and result is established here because the scale of operation is small, and an energetic leader motivated by reward serves as the "whip."

The contract system, therefore, has been a step in the right direction. But it is still beset with problems. There are not enough machines to go around, and household groups are not permitted to lease them from each other. Nor can labor be hired. The contract households are not permitted to deal freely in men and materials with another unit. A major problem, here and there, is a shortage of accountants. The households receive advances at the beginning of the season and get paid, bonus and all, at the end. For this arrangement to be viable, accounts must be maintained regularly and settled at frequent intervals.

The more successful application of the contract system has taken place in livestock rearing, particularly, in the Baltic republics. The households breed and rear the livestock and sell the animals at contracted prices to the farms. The livestock are then resold to state procurement agencies. The households are expected to pay for the fodder and feed according to the terms set out in the contract, but some of these supplies are undoubtedly pilfered from the farm stocks. Where payments are enforced, they are used with economy. Overall, Soviet livestock practices are wasteful and the feed mix is unbalanced: there is an overuse of grain, especially wheat, and an underuse of roughage and pasture. With sluggish production of sunflower seeds, the intake of seed meal is also inadequate. This is being countered by large imports of soybean meal. All in all, Soviet livestock practices have not kept up with the times.

The encouraging performer in agriculture is the private plot. Soviet experts and General Secretary Gorbachev have insisted that "private plot" is a misnomer. It is the small plot, averaging half an acre, that a farm family treats as its own and uses in the way it sees best, raising hogs or chickens or a few dairy cows, growing potatoes and vegetables, or cultivating a fruit orchard. Quite often, it manages to get the materials—for example, seeds or fodder—free. It is difficult, therefore, to estimate the "true" costs of these activities and hence their cost-effectiveness. However, they do supply large amounts of various items, from pork and other meats, eggs, and milk to fresh fruits and vegetables. These are sold in the open collective (*kolkhoz*) markets at prices that truly reflect the vagaries of demand and supply.

Whatever name one chooses to give to these arrangements, they have proved enduring. The private plot was born as a concession to the land-hungry peasantry after its lands and livestock were forcibly collectivized. Khrushchev's attitude to the private plot was vacillating, generous at the start but confiscatory toward the end. With Brezhnev's Food Program (begun in May 1982), which promised an improved and variegated diet to the populace, the role of the private plot was conceded. Under Gorbachev, that role has been affirmed.

SERVICES

The Soviet service sector is also faring poorly. Capitalist economies, by contrast, are marked by proliferating services. Service industries are a dynamic feature of the urbanization process, in the Third World as well as in capitalist countries, providing employment by pulling people from faraway places to the urban centers and enriching daily existence in the process. In the Third World, the trickle started in the fifties and sixties, with household workers, shoeshine boys, newspaper, fruit, and flower vendors at traffic lights, and porters on railway platforms;

it had swollen and diversified by the seventies, and later moved into new ventures—pizza and ice-cream parlors, small dressmaking shops, and, now, the computer training facilities that have replaced the typing services of the past. There is perhaps not much glamor here, but there is a lot of entrepreneurial energy.

In the First World, services take forms at once more glamorous and utilitarian. Restaurants (later discos), hairdressing salons, dry-cleaning services, and taxis number among the traditional types. The modern services include telecommunications, consulting, and financial activities: they are the prime movers of advanced industrial economies.

In a large measure, both these ends of the service spectrum, the ordinary and the extraordinary, have bypassed the Soviet scene—but for different reasons. Around the time Mikhail Gorbachev became General Secretary in March 1985, there were no French or Italian restaurants in Moscow. Bourgeois food was kept out along with bourgeois ideology. Financial, trading, educational, and medical services certainly exist, but they are owned and administered by the state. The results, as can be expected, are shortages, poor quality, lack of variety, and monumental indifference from the service personnel in state outlets. If one is looking for entertainment, there is a profusion of high-brow activities such as going to the ballet, museums, poetry readings, and the censored cinema. Of course, one can always go out for a walk, collect mushrooms, and smell the flowers. But the young hanker for something low-brow and outlandish (perhaps rock in smoke-filled discos or a hot dog at a sidewalk stand), while the old have but limited time for entertainment since they are continually battling the system: just try to get an appliance fixed in Moscow.

One outcome of the shortage, or absence, of services has been the rise of a "second," or "underground," service sector for which there is considerable evidence and even a few estimates. With proper contacts, adequate payments, and ceaseless efforts, one can arrange for repairs, dental work, small paint jobs, and the like. Most of these activities fall outside the official network and are therefore illegal.

FOREIGN TRADE

How do Soviet planners decide what to export, and in what amounts and to which destination? How are items to be imported identified along with their amounts and sources?

FIG. 2.1.   The diversion of planned allocations of materials to the lucrative "second" economy is illustrated in this 1987 *Krokodil* cartoon. Two prosperous comrades, their knapsacks bulging with cement, shower heads, and saw blades, greet each other. One says: "Off to the dacha?" The other replies: "No, I am off to my new apartment." Reprinted, by permission, from *Krokodil*, no. 1 (January 1987).

In a market economy without frictions, commodities and services that can be produced relatively cheaply at home are exported; those that are relatively costly to produce are imported. For this to happen, the value of the currency must be determined by market forces. The resulting exchange rate provides an organic and beneficial link between domestic and external activities. If, at the current rate of exchange, balance of payments surpluses or deficits persist, the exchange rate is generally allowed to change appropriately. While departures from this ideal arrangement are widespread, it is recognized that they should be minimized.

That, however, is not the view of the Soviet planners. Soviet exports and imports, like everything else in the economy, are planned. A plan lays down the amounts of the major items to be produced and the materials and manpower that will be required for the purpose. If a shortfall of a needed item from domestic sources is anticipated, its importation will be planned. On the other hand, if the calculation suggests that the demand for oil during the plan will be less than the oil production for the period, oil exports will be planned. The Soviet Union may reasonably be regarded as being cost-effective in exporting traditional items such as timber and ore. But except for these, the overriding question is: Are the planned exports and imports in keeping with the Soviet Union's "true" costs, that is, with what economists call "comparative advantage"? Soviet planners have indeed been aware of this problem:

> Given distorted [domestic] prices and exchange rates, planners often find themselves without a rational basis for deciding what should and should not be exported or imported. . . . Over the past decade, most of the effort to rationalize foreign trade decisions has gone into the development of so-called foreign trade effectiveness indexes. . . . Basically, they attempt to answer the following questions. In the case of exports, which domestically produced commodities will earn the largest amount of foreign exchange per ruble . . . of expendi-

ture of domestic resources? In the case of imports, which commodities will save the largest amount of domestic resources per dollar of foreign exchange expended? (Holzman 1976, 33–34)

These "effectiveness" ratios cannot be rational if they are based on domestic prices, since these are not market-determined. The Soviet practice is therefore to adjust these prices to calculate the effectiveness ratios. But these adjustments in practice are inadequate to the purpose at hand: there is really no sensible way to guess at the "true" market prices. (For example, suppose the market price of a machine to the domestic user is subsidized and is, therefore, less than its cost of production. The latter is occasionally used as an approximation to the "true" price in calculating the effectiveness ratio. But this amounts to mere ritual, because the prices used for calculating the cost of production are irrational to begin with.)

The institutional arrangement designed to promote foreign trade has been counterproductive, too. Until recently, all foreign trade activities were managed by the Foreign Trade Organizations (FTOs)—a procedure that isolates the actual producing and consuming enterprises from the outside world. Whether an item is sold in the domestic market or to the FTO for export, the producing enterprise receives the domestic wholesale price with a supplement, if necessary, to cover higher costs or a special export bonus. The payment is generally inadequate to cover the additional cost of fulfilling the special requirements of the foreign buyer (Hewett 1988a, 293–94). As for imports, enterprises have little incentive to economize on their use. They pay a wholesale price that is an arbitrary domestic equivalent of the foreign price. In short, the arrangements afford little incentive to generate exports or to use imports sparingly.

Within this setup, a central concern of the planners has been to minimize trade deficits with hard-currency countries. Declining oil prices have exacerbated the situation with the result that less foreign exchange is available for importing machines, scarce metals, and grain. The planners' response, once again, has been typical. Imports from hard-currency areas are allowed when the items are not available from partners in Eastern Europe or the Third World with whom trade is settled on a bilateral and barter basis. Why import a machine from West Germany and pay for it in deutsche marks when a similar machine can be imported from East Germany and paid for in Soviet timber? Why import corn from the United States when it can be imported from Argentina and repaid with exports of Soviet electricity-generating turbines with some oil thrown in?

Despite such caution, actual hard-currency earnings generally fall short of the planned amounts required for purchases from hard-currency sources. There are two solutions to the problem: imports can be cut back with resulting hardships and bottlenecks, or they can be financed at planned levels with hard-currency borrowings. Soviet planners have resorted to both these stratagems in recent years. By the latest count, gross hard-currency debt in 1986 had risen to $38.2 billion (McIntyre 1987a, 482). Debt-servicing liabilities used up about 23 percent of the $25.1 billion in Soviet hard-currency export earnings for 1986 (McIntyre 1987a, 477, 483). This is not a fraction over which Soviet planners should lose sleep. Similar fractions for Brazil and Mexico, which have meant restless nights for their creditors, are currently unmanageable. By contrast, the current Soviet debt-repayment potential is respectable and the actual record is impeccable.

Why have Soviet planners exhibited such caution in their hard-currency borrowings? Their chief concern is the inability to push exports of manufactured items far and fast enough in hard-currency markets, and the consequent worry about servicing large debts. As I have said, the bonanza from zooming oil prices is over. Besides, it is unsafe to rely on the export of a few raw materials; timber, for example, has ceased to be critical in construction. Some of these materials are expensive to extract anyway. As for manufactured exports, the Soviet planners recognized their role in solving the foreign exchange problem. But then there is the special problem of the absence of a level playing field in the U.S. market: the Jackson-Vanik Amendment of 1974 denies Soviet exports the most-favored-nation (MFN) treatment; as a result, potential Soviet exports in American markets face a higher tariff than similar exports from elsewhere. Given their poor quality, Soviet manufactured exports would find it difficult to make headway in U.S. markets and elsewhere in any event.

As the foregoing review underlines, the Soviet economic system that Gorbachev inherited has all the trappings of a rigid institutional structure. Commands from the central planners have left little initiative, and even less incentive, for the performing actors and economic agents. The ill-fitting pieces of shortages, bottlenecks, retarded innovation, and faltering growth have been the inevitable consequences. Gorbachev has chosen to restructure the jigsaw puzzle and provide incentives to the players to fit the pieces where they belong.

The Reforms: Their Design

MIKHAIL GORBACHEV'S REFORMS have been announced in a succession, indeed a blitzkrieg, of decrees. As a result, it is easy to miss the forest for the trees. I will therefore concentrate in this chapter on reviewing the salient features of these decrees, as they relate to the key areas of industry, agriculture, services, and foreign trade. This should pave the way for the critical analysis later (in chapters 5, 6, and 7) of the essential nature of Gorbachev's reforms and, hence, of their promise and prospects.

OUTLINE OF THE ECONOMIC REFORMS

At the outset, it is important to note that the reforms are envisaged as a continuing process. The price reform, for instance, will not begin until 1991. The planners are aware that current prices do not reflect the market forces of supply and demand. For example, the price of oil paid by Soviet consumers, including industrial users, is way below its world price. Consumers buy bread, meat, milk, and several items at prices substantially below their costs to producers. These prices, and many more, must be changed. Annual plans too are expected to cease, beginning in 1991, although plans for five-year and longer periods will continue to be formulated. It is also possible that unanticipated changes in the existing decrees will be announced. My assessment of the economic reforms based on the current package may therefore turn out to be incomplete in view of the fluid situation. Nevertheless, the Soviet planners' perceptions of what ails the economy, what should be the objective of the economic reform, and what plan of action should be devised are abundantly clear.

In the planners' view, the most pressing problem is the declining growth rate of the economy and the mismatching of supplies and demands. The diagnosis is in line with what many analysts have been saying for years: the economy is overplanned and overadministered. The excessive planning (as I indicated in chapter 2) consists of the plethora of targets handed down from above to managers. The overadministration manifests itself in the detailed role of the state apparatus in handling the innumerable production, distribution, and financial transactions of a modern, complex economy.

As a result, Soviet firms and farms have little genuine autonomy and few incentives in matters such as deciding what to produce, which raw materials to procure and from where, how much to sell, what prices to charge, which capacities to scrap and which new machines to install, and which new technologies to develop or adopt. The state wholesale suppliers and retail shops have no incentives to push sales or clear inventories. As for the banks, they essentially support the production and investment activities laid down by the planners and provide the required financing. There are two ways of coping with the system. Those at the top of the managerial hierarchy squander their energies and talents in battling the Kafkaesque maze of bureaucratic controls. The majority at the bottom follow orders with a lackluster handling of their chores, somewhat in the style of Gogol's Akaki Akakievich. In the planners' view, the first priority, therefore, is to make all the actors in production, distribution, and financing truly autonomous and give them appropriate incentives.

There is a related, acute problem that the planners want to address. Because the economy is overplanned and overadministered, the invisible hand of the market is nowhere to be seen. Because the production targets are handed down from above, what is produced has little relation to what is demanded. The economy is characterized by the paradox of excess demand and massive inventories.

Therefore, the plan must gradually recede and increasingly make way for the market.*

But how can autonomy and initiatives in pursuit of profits be encouraged? It is not enough to prohibit the ministries by law from interfering in the day-to-day working of the individual units. It is necessary to create a vigorous environment of debate and discussion of economic issues. Instances of higher-level interference should be aired in public, and managerial performance should be evaluated. Workers should be allowed to elect managers. There is a role for openness (glasnost') and grass-roots democracy here.

What more should be done to handle the problem of lagging production and productivity? The planners see the need for short-term devices and a long-term strategy. Both would be aimed at raising the productivity of the work force. In the short run, there is a role for disciplinary measures so that the widespread goofing-off is brought under control. Workers must at least appear at their work place and carry out their jobs. Absenteeism due to alcoholism must be curbed.† But in the long run, the well-tried remedy for raising productivity is to provide workers with better machines. By all accounts, most of the Soviet capital stock is antiquated. Soviet factories also need greater automation. Soviet machine building capacities must be renovated and automated.

---

* As I will analyze in chapter 5, the Soviet planners' conception of the market differs from the market arrangements that function under a capitalist system.

† Within two months after Gorbachev became General Secretary in March 1985, the prices of alcohol products were raised, shop hours were reduced, and criminal sanctions against drunkenness were tightened. This was followed by reduced production, by command, of alcohol products. As a result, the liquor lines have become longer and *samogon* (illicit brewing) has increased. Recently, there has been some softening; the right to sell beer, wine, and cognac—but, alas, no vodka—was restored to grocery stores via a decree of September 1988.

FIG. 3.1. In this 1987 *Krokodil* cartoon, a bureaucrat with a welcoming smile and a ready hand greets a plaintive citizen: "Congratulations! We have already started processing your request." The letter will travel from hand to hand along a chain of bureaucrats receding into the horizon. The cartoon illustrates the pervasive burden of bureaucracy on the Soviet economy and society. Reprinted, by permission, from the cover of *Krokodil*, no. 10 (April 1987).

The reform package, in the planners' view, must further contend with issues relating to consumerism and equity. While the stress is on growth and efficiency, the reformers also emphasize the need to improve consumption levels and variety, implying therefore that the higher weight traditionally placed on investment relative to consumption must yield to a greater abundance of consumer goods here and now. But the equity issue goes to the very core of the ideology defining the Soviet state. There is now explicit emphasis on rejecting "mindless egalitarianism." The tendency toward the excessive wage leveling of the Brezhnev years is to yield to higher wages for the more productive and the better-trained workers. Rather than reflecting the egalitarian Communist norm, the reward system is to be anchored decisively in the more productive socialist norm: "From each according to his ability, to each according to his work."

Such is the broad outline of the new thinking, which wrestles with the problem, its diagnosis, the prescribed remedy, and the underlying objective of the remedy. As articulated by Mikhail Gorbachev, it spills over into several noneconomic dimensions and acquires a certain grandeur. His perestroika is concerned not merely with the problem of quickening the growth rate (*uskorenie*) of the economy and the technological transformation of Soviet industry for the purpose; he is also arguing for a switch from administrative to economic management. His conception and plan of action go beyond mere economic restructuring. There must be a massive participation of the working men and women in economic decision making in their places of work. There must be suitable incentives and the absence of interference from higher-ups. The give-and-take of views in a general environment of openness (glasnost'), the selection of managers by workers in enterprises, the elections of public officials to local bodies via secret ballot and with a choice of candidates—these are all ingredients of democratization (*demokratizatsiia*). How else can corruption and alienation be wrestled with? His program also extends to a systematic weeding out of the outdated and coercive features of the existing arrangements in law and education. Literature and the arts must be revitalized, too. And the conduct of foreign policy must be brought into the service of this grand mission.

The economic reforms of perestroika announced in successive decrees have been in preparation for quite a while. The government, the party, and the people were drawn in at various levels while the decrees were being drafted. The proposed changes are outlined step by step, in one painstaking paragraph after another. The decrees are typical Soviet documents, heavy with the nuts and bolts of Soviet economic writing, peppered with the dry lexicon of the Marxist-Leninist approach, and relentlessly colorless. The ongoing revolution is thus twice blessed—with Gorbachev's populist appeal and the socialist legality that the decrees embody.

The important pieces of legislation (since Gorbachev became General Secretary) that bear on the economic restructuring and that I will discuss below are the Law on the State Enterprise (Association), which was introduced in mid-1987 to cover the economic activity of all state units; the March 1986 Decree on Agricultural Management, which added momentum to the contract system on the collective farms; the final Law on Cooperatives, which became effective July 1, 1988; and the decree on foreign trading activity and the Law on Joint Ventures that went into effect on January 1, 1987.

How does one wrestle with these documents? A few lines must be read over and over, some parts can be skipped, and reading between the lines, which comes with long practice, is always helpful. What I have distilled below represents, in my view, what is important and relevant.

THE LAW ON THE STATE ENTERPRISE

The Law on the State Enterprise (Association) (hereafter, the Law) relates to all producing, processing, financing, distributing, and trading units in the state sector. Not only the industrial enterprises but also the State Bank and the Investment Bank, the state farms, and the state sales outlets are included under its provisions. Also included are the associations whose members undertake various stages of manufacturing activity, or R & D and manufacturing, under one roof. Not included are the collective farms, the cooperative sales outlets, and the rest of the cooperative sector.

The Law proposes several changes in the current working arrangements of state enterprises. These are to be carried out by the end of 1990. Except for the important products for which they will be given state orders (*goszakazy*), enterprises will be left free to select their output plan based on contracts with other units. The state orders, for which materials are to be allotted, must be fulfilled. As for the materials for the contracts, they can be procured from the supplying enterprises at prices that are allowed to move within limits. The caveat on price flexibility is necessary because, according to Abel Aganbegyan (1988, 118), the enterprises are currently awash in liquidity: they have been borrowing freely from the State Bank and have been in no hurry to repay the loans because interest charges are not enforced.

While the straitjacket on production activity is thus to be loosened, financial responsibility, autonomy, and incentives are also envisaged in enterprise management. As I have already noted, financial accountability via khozraschet has thus far been a cost-accounting ritual: the state has bailed out losing enterprises with the result that the budget constraint, in effect, has been "soft." The Law plans to make it "hard." The enterprises must become self-financing (*samofinansirovannye*). "The enterprise is explicitly enjoined to maximize net revenues after meeting the cost of supplies, contributing to the central and local budgets and its ministry, and paying for credit [Articles 2, 3 and 17]" (Ericson 1988, 5). The Law also has provisions for insolvency so that an enterprise can be declared bankrupt and dissolved.

As for enterprise autonomy, it is to be achieved through a greater role for the worker collective, which consists of the entire work force in an enterprise. The worker collective will elect a council and the enterprise manager. The distribution of the funds at the disposal of the enterprise between payments to managers and workers, between long-term goals such as investment, product innovation, and development on the one hand and "consumption" (such as housing) on the other, is to be decided by the council. The intention of the Law is not to force choices on the enterprises but merely to "guide" them.

Finally, what about financial incentives for managers and workers? According to Aganbegyan (1988, 117), enterprises in a given branch are to be taxed at uniform rates. Thus, the differential rates at which enterprises were taxed earlier (with the more profitable among them paying higher rates) will eventually be done away with. Enterprise efficiency is thus to be rewarded and encouraged, along with higher labor productivity. The more productive workers are to be rewarded, over and above their wage scales, by additional payment, payment in kind, or extra leave. As on the collective farms, the better-performing work brigades will receive higher compensation for fulfilling the production tasks for which they have contracted with the enterprise management.

But certainly there are limits to enterprise autonomy. They will continue to impinge on enterprises in several ways.

First, there are the economic norms set by the planners. Suppose an enterprise "maximizes its net revenue." How much it retains and how much it surrenders to the state are prescribed by the relevant norm. Then there are norms "guiding" the distribution of retained earnings among such uses as investment and social consumption—for example, housing financed by enterprises. Planners continue to decide what "major" projects are to be set up because they know best: the enterprises are to be left alone to innovate and invest only in the remaining projects, which add up to a small fraction of total investment.

What about the role of the ministries? In the compelling words of the general manager of a machine-building plant at the June Party Conference: "No where else in the world are there so many ministries. . . . To tell you the truth, we do not need ministries. . . . We earn our own keep. We earn our own hard currency. What can they give us? Nothing. . . . Let the ministries catch mice. If they don't, they do not get to eat" (*Pravda*, July 1, 1988). What does the Law propose to do about the situation? One would have thought that the umbilical cord with the ministries would finally be severed. But the ministries are still to be "held responsible for satisfaction of demand for their products, for productivity increases, for product quality, product and process innovation in their branch, and for the maintenance of a progressive capital structure" (Ericson 1988, 8).

Finally, within the enterprise, there are limits on the freedom of enterprise managers that arise from the powers of the worker collective and its council. "If management disagrees with the council, the matter is referred to the general meeting of the labor collective, whose decision binds not only management and its own membership, but also superior State and economic agencies (so long as the decision is not illegal)" (Butler 1988, 7). The decision of the manager to hire or transfer a worker must also be approved by the brigade council.

THE COLLECTIVE FARMS

What reforms were proposed for the collective farms in the March 1986 decree?

The decree contained an explicit measure for providing incentives to collective farms. The farms are free to sell a certain fraction of their above-quota surpluses in cooperative and private outlets where the prices are generally higher than official prices. The official procurement agencies get the rest. How best to procure agricultural produce from the farms for use by the urban population has been a perennial problem for Soviet leaders from the days of Lenin. Gorbachev announced at the twenty-seventh Party Congress in February 1986 that the Leninist innovation of *prodnalog* (the food tax) should be adopted "creatively" for the purpose. This announcement aroused great expectations: What did the General Secretary have in mind? The implication of his suggestion was that instead of being asked to fulfill procurement quotas at fixed prices, the collective farms would be given the incentive to dispose of their above-quota surpluses at higher-than-official prices. And what better way to advance the idea than by invoking Lenin? During the years of War Communism (1918–1921), when the towns were ravaged and hungry, grain was forcibly extracted from the peasants. The peasants responded by concealing harvests and reducing plantings. The forced and arbitrary procurement was abandoned in March 1921 on Lenin's initiative and replaced by a proportional agricultural tax: a fixed proportion of the net produce was taxed, with the tax rate differentiated by the size of the peasant family and its landholdings. The assurance that only a fixed share of the net surplus would be taxed away left the peasants with the incentive to maximize their surplus. More than six decades later, on Gorbachev's initiative, the incentive effect of the idea of prodnalog is being directed at Soviet collective farms.

Several provisions of the March 1986 decree were in the nature of exhortations—that is, the farms should be self-financing, they should divert investments downstream to storage and marketing rather than into machinery purchases, and so on. The decree, however, endorsed the contract system noted earlier in which households on the collective farm can band together and undertake various activities in line with the terms specified in their contract with the farm management. The critical question here is, How can these households be truly autonomous if contracts are specified for them by the collective farm management? From this perspective, the reform of collective farms has proved vexing for Gorbachev and his planners. Let me discuss this point by contrasting the reforms in Chinese and Hungarian agriculture with the absence of similar action in the Soviet Union.

The reforms of agriculture in China marked a total about-face from Mao's agrarian revolution. The communes were disbanded in the midseventies, land was handed over to the peasants for a period of fifteen years, and output targets were abolished. Labor can now be hired, and land can be bought and sold. Reforms in Hungarian agriculture, which began in the sixties, were brought about differently. The state made a substantial investment in agriculture, and farm cooperatives were formed. The activities of the cooperatives cover everything in the rural economy—the production of crops and livestock products, including their processing; the repair and maintenance of equipment and buildings; and construction work and small-scale industries. The targets from the planners are flexible, and the cooperatives can buy and sell from each other at mutually acceptable prices. Within the guidelines of these targets, the cooperatives are truly autonomous.

Which reform route can and will the Soviet planners take? A wholehearted embrace of the Chinese road is ideologically hazardous and technologically difficult. If land is actually restored to the peasants, then state ownership of other means of production may have to be given up too. In their forward march to capitalism, the Chinese planners have dropped the baggage of public ownership of the means of production—at least in the agricultural sector. "It does not matter if the cat is black or white so long as it catches mice" is by now a threadbare acknowledgment of the pragmatic thrust of Chinese reform. By contrast, the color of the cat is of concern to the Soviet planners. Moreover, the Chinese plots are small and Chinese agriculture is labor-intensive. The change does not create vast demands for industrial items such as tractors, machines, spare parts, and the like, which can upset the plan in industry. Soviet farms, on the other hand, would remain large and capital-intensive even after their dissolution (this is because the population density is much lower).

While the Russian bear cannot follow the panda, can it take the Hungarian route? This could imply that the contract brigades and links would be permitted to lease the land directly from the state rather than from the collective farm and to cultivate it as their own, and that they could sell their produce to other cooperatives and buy materials and machines directly from industrial enterprises. A brigade that produces tomatoes could sell them directly to a tomato-processing cooperative without having to go through the collective farm intermediation as at present. The brigade could hire the services of a building cooperative for repairs and construction. If industrial enterprises contracted directly with other enterprises, why couldn't farm cooperatives deal directly with one another and with industrial enterprises? This could set in motion economy-wide demands for machines and materials—a possibility the Soviet planners would like to avoid. (On the other hand, it may result in more efficient use of the current capital stock.) Then again, some cooperatives would prosper more than others.

Whatever the reasons, perestroika in agriculture has been slow. It has not exhibited the Chinese chutzpah or the Hungarian resoluteness. The initial view of reform was that incentives for better performance should be provided to farm households within the existing institutional arrangement. The formation of contracts by the farm management with the links and brigades was to continue. Subsequently, along the lines of the Chinese family responsibility system, an individual family was allowed to form a contract. Presumably, the family contract (*semeinyi podriad*) is an arrangement in which a farm family signs a contract with the collective farm management to deliver something, perhaps livestock; by contrast, the link and brigade contracts involve a group of families. The family contract is currently being touted with great fanfare: the front page of *Izvestiia* displays occasionally the picture of a cheerful farm family that has set a record in rearing hogs. (What is the difference between the family contract and the private plot? As I have noted, the family is free to do what it pleases with the private plot. However, it may need to form a contract with the farm for getting livestock feed or using the farm truck for transporting, say, potatoes from the plot to the nearest kolkhoz market. There is not much difference here between the private plot and the family contract.)

Recently, Gorbachev has proposed measures which can gradually loosen the institutional setting of the Soviet farm. He suggested to the Central Committee (*Pravda*, July 29, 1988) that a special law should be enacted allowing farmers to lease land for "25, 30 and even 50 years." In mid-October 1988, he called for the promotion of farms leased to families across the country without explicitly stating that the collective and state farms be dissolved. However, the implication of his suggestion was that the collective and state farm management might recede into the background, perhaps in the role of service agencies, if individual farming on leased plots took hold. In order for these proposals to be effective, they have to be formally enacted into a decree.

THE LAW ON COOPERATIVES

While reforms in the collective farm sector are moving ahead, they are marching in quick succession in the cooperative sector. I discussed earlier the dismal state of services in the economy and the prevalence of the "second" economy in coping with the shortages. The obvious remedy for the situation is for the lawmakers to legalize the second economy.

The first stage of the reforms, which became effective in May 1987, proposed to do that without explicitly saying so. The provision of individual labor activity (*individual'naia trudovaia deiatel'nost*) was invoked to allow private and co-operative businesses such as restaurants, auto-repair services, private taxis, and small manufacturing operations. However, there were restrictions on entry into these activities. Only retired people and people without a job, such as housewives, could band together for the purpose. State employees could avail themselves of these opportunities only in off-hours. A license, requiring a fee, had to be obtained from the local authorities to start a private or cooperative venture. The next step came in September 1987 when the law was extended to include privately run shops and the use of space in state stores for selling goods and produce. Even while the cooperatives were beginning to take hold in a few service areas, the leveling instincts of the planners asserted themselves in a tax law that became effective on April 1, 1988. Taxes were imposed on a sliding scale, rising to 90 percent, on incomes earned from cooperative ventures. When Prime Minister Ryzhkov presented the draft of a new law on cooperatives two months later in the Supreme Soviet, he found himself battling a tax revolt among the normally pliant members. The taxes, some deputies argued, were not only a disincentive but infringed on the rights of local governments to provide tax breaks to businesses. While consideration of amending or abrogating the tax measure was put off to a future date, the legislature passed the new Law on Cooperatives, which went into effect on July 1, 1988. Cooperatives are now free to engage in any activity including banking and foreign trade. They can sell shares and set up joint ventures with foreign companies. There are to be no limits on who joins a cooperative, its size, the industry or service it chooses to enter or start, and the earnings of members, which can be distributed in proportion to their share of investment as well as their effort. The cooperatives do not need special permission from local authorities, although their compulsory registration in many places continues. They are free to hire full-time employees and set prices for their products and services. Finally, the monkey on their backs was removed on July 29 when the Presidium of the Supreme Soviet abolished the tax law.

The Foreign Sector

The proposed changes provide some initiative and incentive for enterprises and associations in foreign trading activities and specify the guidelines for foreign equity participation.

The law on foreign trading activities grants direct trading rights to twenty ministries and seventy production associations and enterprises. The intention is to remove the surveillance of the FTO "nanny." In the absence of markets that automatically pick up tradable items, the planners have identified agencies and activities that are to promote exports. Since the objective is to encourage manufactured exports, machine-building industries feature prominently in the list (McIntyre 1987b, 498). Depending on the product, enterprises can retain up to half of their foreign exchange earnings in their accounts with the Foreign Trade Bank (Vneshtorgbank) and use them for buying machines and know-how from abroad so that their production capacities can be modernized and their products exported. Failure to meet export commitments can result in reduced allocations of foreign exchange.

The provisions relating to foreign equity participation, long in the making and eagerly awaited, went into effect on January 1, 1987. Here the interest of the foreign partner and the desire of the Soviet planners are truly divergent. The former wants to tap the huge excess demands of a high-income society for a variety of items, among them consumer goods; the latter wants foreign technology, with the related manufacturing and managerial expertise, in order to produce exports and items for domestic use that are currently imported. The Soviet goal is foreign exchange earnings; the foreigner's goal is making profits in Soviet markets. The job now is to arrive at the optimum give-and-take.

The guidelines are still evolving but there is an outline: The basic idea is that foreign participation should not create net hard-currency liabilities. This is the bottom line that will apply to each joint venture. Let me illustrate the severity of this constraint with an example. Two innovative American businessmen decided to introduce Moscow residents to the pleasure of the pizza pie. They needed to import a mobile van with pizza-making equipment, as well as the ingredients. However, they had to find a way of recovering the dollar cost of the imports. They might, for example, have bought Ukrainian handicrafts and exported them abroad. They decided instead to sell part of the pizza output in a couple of hotels where the tourists must pay in dollars for a piece of genuine American pizza in Moscow.

The provisions of the joint venture legislation are guided by this overriding consideration. The foreign partner, with equity participation of up to 49 percent, is to provide equipment, technology, and the required foreign exchange financing, while the Soviet side contributes "social infrastructure." Profits can be repatriated at a 50-percent tax rate. By contrast, the tax rate on retained profits is 30 percent (McIntyre 1987b, 500; Gurevich 1987, 1–4). (There are recent reports [*New York Times*, October 29, 1988] that foreign companies may be allowed to own more than 50 percent of a joint venture and take their profits out with less difficulty, but exact details of the proposed changes are not available.) Are Soviet enterprises free to initiate and negotiate joint venture arrangements with Western partners? That role is apparently assigned to a state agency (Gurevich 1987, 1–4). However, enterprises are free to establish direct ties and negotiate various features of an arrangement, such as prices and product mix, with a CMEA (Council for Mutual Economic Assistance) partner (*Pravda*, September 24, 1986).

Naturally, the provisions relating to the management of the joint ventures are intended to satisfy the specific requirements of their socialist host. The board of directors will be mixed, but the chairman and director general must be local. Soviet laws must be followed with regard to the employment conditions of the work force, but the really critical issues of the foreign partner's authority to reduce wages, fire employees, and close the operation have been left unsettled.

Will the ruble be made convertible in the near future? There are no plans in sight to do so, although pronouncements appear now and then. Under current arrangements, the exchange rate is irrelevant in the settlement of foreign trading activities. Soviet-American trade is conducted in dollars, and surpluses and deficits are settled in dollars. There is no need here for a ruble-dollar conversion rate. However, given the limited potential of selling in American markets and earning dollars, a dollar deficit is kept to the minimum. One result is that Soviet citizens are not allowed to convert rubles into dollars. As for Soviet-CMEA trade, it is conducted in world prices; however, since trade is balanced bilaterally to a "very fine degree," surpluses and deficits are not allowed to develop for long. This managed trade regime clearly implies that foreign importers (except tourists) cannot be allowed to shop indiscriminately in the Soviet market:

> Basically, they are restricted to those products offered by the FTOS as established in the annual plans, most of which have already been preempted in one of the foreign trade agreements. There are two major reasons for this form of restriction on potential buyers. First, unplanned purchases by foreign importers would disrupt the carefully drawn fabric of the plan implemented by balances and other direct controls. Second, given irrational prices, importers might purchase commodities at prices far below the real costs of production (for example, heavily subsidized commodities). For these reasons, the Communist countries do not allow foreigners to hold their curren-

cies (or convert them freely into goods). Even if they did allow their currencies to be held externally, there would not be any takers because of the great uncertainties as to what the money could buy, if anything, and at what price. (Holzman 1976, 43)

What then is the role of the exchange rate? The official price of the ruble with respect to the dollar serves an accounting role: imports in dollar values are converted into rubles for calculating the balance of trade. An exchange rate, which can deviate from this accounting unit, is also necessary for facilitating the local outlays of tourists and diplomats. In reality, the market price of the ruble depends on whether one is offering jeans or videocassettes on Moscow streets. But these kinds of highly publicized goods are the tip of an iceberg. Soviet demands for items from hard-currency markets, if left unchecked, are likely to go through the roof, whereas the demands of the hard-currency consumers for Soviet goods are modest. This implies that the supply of rubles by Soviet purchasers far exceeds the demand for rubles by outsiders. The ruble is not a valuable currency to own. If it were made convertible now, the emperor would be left without his clothes.

The Likelihood of Success: 1965 versus Now

IN EVALUATING the merits of the reforms,[1] the first logical step, in my view, is to assess the chances of their success by contrasting them with the 1965 reforms, which did not succeed.

On paper, the reforms of 1965 under the Kosygin-Brezhnev leadership were a big step forward. They represented the first attempt at toning up enterprise performance by giving it financial incentives. They also addressed the problems of improving product quality and introducing new technologies into the economy. There were reforms in agriculture, and prices were revised too.

The 1965 reforms were precursors of the current package in one notable regard. As now, there was discussion among academics, led by Evsey Liberman at the time, of the need for changing enterprise management and the role of profit in spearheading the process. The commission that was appointed within the Academy of Sciences for working out the reform proposals consisted among others of Nemchinov, Kantorovich, and Abel Aganbegyan himself. Aganbegyan's reminiscences (1988, 58) of the period are brief but telling. The issues under consideration were wide-ranging and challenging. Shouldn't interest charges be included as the cost of capital in prices? What should be the role of profit in managerial decision making? Shouldn't there be wholesale trade in materials and machines instead of planned allocation and distribution?

The economists had their way. For the first time, profits and sales became performance rules for enterprises, in addition to gross output (val). Capital charges were also introduced, not as part of the cost of production but as payment out of profits to the state budget. The limit on the overall wage bill in the enterprise plan was retained, but enterprise management was left free to reallocate the work force. This implied that the average wage rate, labor productivity, and the average cost of production were left to the discretion of enterprises. Part of an enterprise's profits was handed over to the state budget, and the remainder was allocated for bonus payments, welfare improvement of the workers, and, most important, for financing technical improvements initiated by the enterprise. Enterprises were enjoined to form associations (*ob'edineniia*) combining research and production, or various stages of production, under one roof. Prices were revised from their 1955 levels according to the "cost plus" rule. Two provisions here were noteworthy. First, procurement prices of most agricultural products were revised upward, largely to accommodate high-cost farms. Second, enterprises were allowed to charge higher-than-prevailing prices on new products; the intention here was to promote quality improvement.

Such, in a nutshell, were the 1965 reform provisions. At the end of more than two decades, the judgment is universal that they failed. There were two shortcomings in the reform package. First, the overall plan and the output targets were retained. The enterprises may have wanted to go by the profits and sales rules, but the ministries, which were responsible for ensuring that the plan was fulfilled in terms of output targets, would not leave them alone. The "petty tutelage" persisted, and val survived intact. On top of this, the associations in between the ministries and enterprises turned out to be an additional authority in the hierarchy; Soviet enterprises lacked the tradition of independence, and their rights of decision making were not legally guaranteed. Second, the profit rule failed to provide sufficient incentive because, in practice, the better performers were taxed at higher rates while the laggards got by with lower tax rates. The profit motive turned out to be an illusion. The enterprises used the new provisions to their advantage as best they could. They charged higher prices, but the products only looked as if they had been improved. They trimmed and rearranged the work force, but with no gains in labor productivity. The sole result was a rise in the average wage rate.

The Gorbachev reform package incorporates the lesson (learned from the 1965 reforms) that, unless plan targets are made flexible and enterprise independence is guaranteed by law and constraints, the mere setting of financial targets and rules (such as profits) will not do the trick. In a socialist system, the planners will not pack up and go home. There are critical areas such as heavy industry and infrastructure in which the planned targets will continue to prevail. With these exceptions, however, the enterprises are now to be left on their own when working out contracts with users of their products, and when procuring materials directly from suppliers at prices that are allowed to vary within limits.

Yet another departure from the 1965 reforms is the realization (Aganbegyan 1988, 116–17) that enterprise profits should be taxed at a uniform rate. Enterprises will have the incentive to make profits because larger amounts can be retained for their own use. Again, the legal sanctions safeguarding enterprise independence, the give-and-take of views in the media on economic matters, and the provision of managerial elections by workers are designed to forestall ministerial activism and managerial passivity in enterprise affairs.

More than all this, however, the current reforms embody the wisdom that a drastic shift of economic gears is not merely a matter of economic science. It has also to be a feat of social engineering and of political craftsmanship. To succeed, perestroika has to be conceived and implemented as a social experiment in which millions participate. At the very least, the notion of change must be acceptable to them before they get involved in what Gorbachev calls a revolution. After the prolonged alienation and corruption of the Brezhnev years, what could be more welcome than a new beginning, a fresh breeze? But change cannot be imposed from above; people will not participate unless they are actively prepared for it. A distinct departure from the introduction of the 1965 reforms is therefore not only the extensive participation of various agencies in preparing the reforms but the creation of a suitable environment for their acceptance when they are unveiled. Aganbegyan (1988, 109) reveals that several agencies were involved at various stages in working out the reforms: "The Law on State Enterprises was drafted by a large group of specialists including directors of enterprises and academics. The project was based on nationwide discussion, which drew upon 180,000 suggestions, additions and proposed amendments. A special commission worked hard to consider these suggestions. The draft law was, as a result, substantially re-worked and then submitted for discussion to the Central Committee." Currently, the details of the price reforms are being hammered out. Leonid Abalkin, who is a prominent participant, talks about the need for psychological preparedness before the retail price of bread and meat can be raised. Gorbachev is contributing actively to the process. The bread and meat subsidies, he says, promote not only waste but inequity. Children play with bread rolls in back alleys and peasants feed them to pigs. As for meat, it is the better-off families that consume more meat and therefore profit from the subsidies. If these prices are raised, the fixed-income pensioners and lowest-level wage earners will be adequately compensated. The removal of these subsidies is not eagerly awaited but it is certainly anticipated, and no one will be surprised when they are rescinded.

A particularly useful public relations feature of the reform debates is the opinion polls. They may not all be scientific, and they do not cover every topic, but they are certainly multiplying. These surveys provide public reaction to the economic features of perestroika and suggest changes in the program's direction and pace. In the process, ideas emerge for new legislation. What areas of activity are to be covered by cooperatives? How is the licensing fee for starting a cooperative to be set? And all the time, Mikhail Gorbachev is on the move, asking questions, answering queries, and reporting to the Politburo.

Evidently, therefore, the reforms are being crafted with insight and promoted with deliberation. But perhaps the most striking aspect of the care and caution with which Gorbachev is proceeding is his insistence that the reforms are based on the ideology and legacy of socialism. Gorbachev cannot afford to be seen walking over to Jeremy Bentham and Milton Friedman's corner. To assure popular consent, he also needs to ground his reforms in a vision of Soviet society that does not reject the revolutionary history of today's Soviet Union or its "essential" correctness. As it happens, Gorbachev's beliefs are consonant with what political prudence would require. As a good Communist, he cannot accept reforms that would deny the legitimacy of socialism itself.

The General Secretary therefore insists that perestroika must draw from the positive aspects of Soviet history. It is not necessary, for this purpose, to go further back than 1917. But there is a problem here. Soviet history from that fateful year on has been full of turmoil and pain. Choosing what should be accepted and what should be avoided in formulating an ideological base for perestroika is a daunting task. Gorbachev's (1987, 38–59; *Pravda*, November 3, 1987) approach to the problem is workmanlike: he turns the pages, one by one, accepting those lessons which are positive and reevaluating those which are negative.

Indeed, the positive and the negative, in his judgment, are so intertwined as to be inseparable. There were "mistakes" under Stalin that resulted from the excesses of the cult of personality; however, the performance of the economy was marked by acceleration (uskorenie) and the growth of heavy industry. Above all, Stalin's leadership saw the country through the dark agony of World War II. What about collectivization? Collectivization was implemented harshly, but it put Soviet agriculture on the threshold of new technology; it became possible to cultivate the collective farms mechanically. Khrushchev's record, too, was colored with pluses and minuses: "winds of change" blew over the country and millions of people were restored to their innocence and dignity. But Khrushchev was a poor administrator. His economic schemes were tinged with "voluntarism" and "subjectivism." Stripped of socialist jargon, they were harebrained. Under Brezhnev, the Soviet Union emerged as a superpower, but the growth of the economy slowed from plan to plan and moral and social values declined even more.

Therefore, Gorbachev's contention, even conviction, is that socialism really did not get a fair chance. The first socialist revolution was carried out under Lenin's leadership, but socialism was practiced after his death under abnormal conditions and in an abnormal way. It is a humane doctrine that speaks out against exploitation and strives for the economic betterment of everyone. "The God that failed" judgment should be directed not against socialism but against the way it was practiced. Gorbachev (1987, 129) truly believes that socialism can promote democracy as well as economic efficiency.

It is this socialist conviction that gives an indigenous content to perestroika. It would seem that Gorbachev has finally managed to resolve the historical conflict between the "Slavophils" and the "Westernizers" in charting an appropriate course for the country. One may borrow Western technology, especially in areas where the Soviet Union is lagging. But the trappings of capitalism, among them the private ownership of the means of production and capitalist political values, are to be kept out. Soviet society will instead devise "socialist democracy," "socialist pluralism," "socialist competition," "socialist incentives," and the like. This is not to deny that the young are enamored of everything American, from jeans to jazz, and crave more freedom of choice, while the old snap up Western books and magazines. Aganbegyan, too, talks favorably about Western management practices. But when all is said and done, there is no denying that the ethos of the land and of the leadership is socialist. And perestroika has to be woven with socialist strands for it to be accepted.

Nowhere is the resulting dilemma of efficient, as distinct from feasible, reform so visible as in the relationship of the perestroika reforms just described to the proper workings of a market mechanism. As I argue in chapter 5, the result is to impart a basic flaw into the economic efficiency of the reform design: the perestroika package lacks the essential ingredients necessary to create workable markets, which are the basis for the efficiency of capitalist systems. To see this, however, it is necessary to begin by considering how markets do work to advantage in capitalist economies.

Introducing Markets: A Faulty Design

A CRITICAL FEATURE of a capitalist market is the freedom to choose. For the consumer, the freedom goes beyond the textbook example of whether one will buy an apple or an orange. "Shall we buy a car or have a baby?" is a consumption decision. "Shall we buy government bonds or IBM stock?" reflects concern over the form savings should take. For the producer, the decisions relate to the amount and assortment of outputs to be produced at given prices and, quite often, to the price itself, anticipating how much a rival would charge on a similar product. The long-term decisions relate to whether capacities should be curtailed or expanded or shut down altogether. For example, there is no way an organization can stay in business if it consistently loses money; it must leave the market before long.

Both the consumers and the producers make decisions in environments that differ sharply from the days of Adam Smith. Consumers can spend more than they earn, and the choice of living beyond one's means extends to the types of credit cards to acquire. The production activity also affords diverse choices: how much money to borrow and how much to raise by floating stocks are the major financial decisions. In these days of corporate capitalism, the garage-based start-up firm is becoming increasingly rare. In fact, small may not only be not beautiful, but it may not be feasible; quite a few technologies demand large-scale production. The industrial world's R & D, its innovation in both processes and products is done in giant enterprises that cannot normally be owned by a person or a small group. The ownership is spread among shareholders who can sell their equity on the stock market if they so desire. The stock market, therefore, plays a critical role in channeling industrial investments.

The other key feature of a market is competition. Adam Smith observed that to keep markets competitive, the natural propensity of businessmen to congregate and cartelize must be curbed. Trust-busting derives from these early fears and precepts. Open international markets are also a guarantor of competition. Developing countries with exchange and trade controls automatically protect domestic producers; in the process, they have often created and nurtured domestic monopolies in sheltered markets, missing out on the benefits of competition.

While freedom of choice and the rigors of competition improve economic efficiency, they do not guarantee job security. Nor do they mean that the associated income distribution will be ethically attractive. Income distribution in market economies is often far from equal, rendering competition hazardous and free choice meaningless for most. The market is a sound allocative device but distinctly inegalitarian.

Capitalist systems cope with the problem of ethics in a world of economic efficiency by seeking equity through politics. Representative democracy, pluralism, and individualism are held to be the political preconditions of economic liberalism. The benign welfare state provides redistribution and the safety net.

The Marxist tradition rejects the possibility of such a benign state. Rather, it would re-create the economy so as to eliminate private ownership and centralize economic decision making, with a view to ensuring egalitarian, ethically attractive outcomes to begin with. Ethics then dominates economic efficiency, whereas with capitalism it is the other way around.

In actual practice, the ethical concerns of the socialist state have expanded from protection of the interests of the proletariat to promotion of the welfare of the population. The safety net not only includes job security, adequate compensation, and safe working conditions, but provisions for free education and medical treatment, cheap housing, subsidized food, and retirement benefits for everyone.

Inheriting this full-blooded socialist tradition, Gorbachev and his planners are prisoners of a mode of thinking about the economic system that cannot readily encompass the true functions of the capitalist market. Nor can they appreciate the preconditions for its successful functioning. This failure of comprehension has led to the conceptual weakness of the reform design.

Let me note straightaway the important features of markets that the current reforms exclude:

1. Private ownership of the means of production is not to be permitted. State ownership is to continue, with the exception of cooperative arrangements in which they will be collectively owned. Means of production can also be leased by an individual from the state.
2. The hiring of an individual by another is not permitted except in a cooperative framework.
3. There are no plans to set up a stock market where stocks can be bought and sold.
4. The decision to start new factories, especially in heavy industry and infrastructure, is kept with the planners.
5. The plan will persist for the items regarded as critical by the planners. Targets for these items will continue, although they will now be called state orders (goszakazy).

All in all, therefore, the reforms are not designed to promote the free entry of resources into an activity in quite the same way as in a market system.

In examining the consequences of these and other departures from conventional market procedures I will discuss industry, agriculture, the cooperative sector, and foreign trade, in that order.

INDUSTRY

The new elements in industry are the rights of enterprises to form contracts with potential buyers; to buy and sell materials at wholesale prices, which can vary within limits; and to make profits. Earlier, enterprises could only produce to planned targets and were allotted materials for that purpose. The key question is: Does the new regime reflect how a market would function? Not really, in my view.[2]

First, there is the problem of having to cope with state orders. At the June Party Conference, Comrade Romazanov, a steelworker from a metallurgical combine, voiced his exasperation over the state order set at 100 percent of the combine output (*Pravda*, July 1, 1988). Equally critical is Gorbachev's view of state orders: "It is most intolerable that enterprises are being forced via state orders to produce goods that are not in demand, forced for the simple reason that they [the ministries] want to fulfill the infamous 'gross output' targets" (*Pravda*, June 29, 1988). These state orders are no different from the output targets of yesteryear: they are obligatory. If a manager rejects them, he will no longer be despatched to Siberia or the psychiatric ward; but he will certainly not be allowed to continue exercising the privilege of denial. The profitability criterion thus has a dagger driven through its heart. The problem will continue to plague all industry, with the single exception of cooperative ventures in light industry exempted from its incidence.

Second, there is a yet more compelling constraint that separates the reformed economic regime from a genuine market. Leaving aside the obligatory state contracts, the Soviet enterprises are now to operate on the basis of "demand-determined" contracts.

These "demand-determined" contracts, however, cannot really simulate the market in capitalist economies. They are no more than made-to-order contractual commitments between state-owned enterprises. By contrast, a large amount of capitalist production is in anticipation of sales and is followed by aggressive salesmanship combined with a search for new markets. In the dynamic Schumpeterian version of the market economy, the producer can actually create a market. The producer gets an idea, anticipates demand, and then proceeds to tailor his production and sales strategy to fulfill the demand for the product based on his idea. Take the VCR market, for exam-

Fig. 5.1. This 1988 *Krokodil* cartoon illustrates the continuing, heavy burden on enterprises of fulfilling state orders handed down by ministries. The gargantuan figure parachuting from a plane marked "Ministry" is titled "State Orders" and provokes the outcry from the terrified factory managers: "Watch out! Our enterprise cannot possibly cope with him!" Reprinted, by permission, from *Krokodil*, no. 16 (June 1988).

ple. Capitalist entrepreneurs operate in an environment of changing technology and taste. Profit seeking has a distinct meaning in this environment, and markets play a central role in this organizational setup. Simply asking the state-owned enterprises to enter into contracts with one another and expecting that markets will be created in a capitalist sense is to misunderstand the workings of capitalism and markets. This is a distortion that is excusable for economists untutored in the workings of capitalism, but it is not without serious consequences for the design of the reform package.

This failure also signifies that the introduction of profits as a criterion for the survival or prosperity of enterprises will not have the same meaning of efficiency found in capitalist systems. Unless the flux and flexibility characteristic of capitalist markets are permitted, with extensive freedom to choose suppliers and buyers and to select product variety as demand and profits require, the heavy hand of state orders and "demand-determined" contracts will lead to a latter-day version of accounting, rather than social, profits.

In fact, the architects of the economic reforms exhibit the related failure to grasp the distinction between economic efficiency and technical efficiency—a distinction that my first-year graduate students learn at the outset but that is not the natural way to think about efficiency problems, as most teachers of economics discover. Thus Abel Aganbegyan (1988, chap. 4) cites many examples of machines that would save fuel and materials. But whether they should be installed is a decision that must be made in light of economic efficiency and not technical norms.[3] Once again, the long-ingrained habits of thinking in terms of technical performance criteria are unlikely to be eliminated in one masterstroke. The primeval instincts of the socialist planner are to search for improved technological performance. Therefore, attempts at enforcing the profit criterion, imperfect as it is, will encounter deep-seated, knee-jerk hostility as reforms are implemented.

AGRICULTURE

The agricultural reforms are gaining momentum. By all accounts, the contract system is spreading. Gorbachev's latest proposals to lease farms to households for up to fifty years have aroused great expectations. He has declared that the peasant should be made the master of the land. The Gorbachev proposal, however, falls short of dissolving the collective farms.

Even though Gorbachev does not currently seem to contemplate decollectivization, the proposed leases could be an improvement over the contract system. They should permit more flexibility in choices such as crop mix, enabling the farm families, for instance, to respond better to market demand than when the collective farm management tells them what to produce. Leases would also give families the incentive to make improvements that, under a contract, could lead to returns that do not necessarily accrue to the families. The only obligation of the family leasing land, under ideal circumstances, should be to pay rent to the collective farm, while critical decisions on production and investment would be left to its own better judgment.

It is important to note however that, while Gorbachev expects the lease system to spread under his program, he does not believe that it is necessary to make it universal. The reason why he expects Soviet agriculture to have diverse economic arrangements is that some collective farms, even under the contract arrangement, are considered to be efficient. Thus, in the Baltic republics and Belorussia in the north, energetic farm families appear to have weakened the collective farm's oppressive managerial role. Gorbachev does not therefore consider it necessary to alter the collective arrangement. As a result, the Soviet agricultural scene may evolve in the direction of collective farms with contracts in regions where the system is supposed to work, and a spread of leases in areas where the system does not work. These latter, inefficient collective farms where Gorbachev wants to introduce the leases rapidly are mostly in the vast Russian republic. Here, there are several farms with few male members and many women and children; others are known to carry the deadweight of a lazy and unmotivated "nonworking majority." The introduction of leases for individual families should eliminate the suffocating effect that these factors impose on those who want to work harder for their own benefit and to the country's advantage.

In considering either system, however—the collective farms where contracts work reasonably well or farms where leases are to be introduced—the same question arises: How do these arrangements relate to the way in which markets function in capitalist societies? The answer is, not too well. The families who operate under the contract system are not generally permitted to buy materials (e.g., fertilizers) or rent equipment (e.g., harvesting machines) freely from others, for instance. As for the emerging lease system, it is likely that similar restrictions may carry over since the collective farms will remain in place (in China, on the other hand, the communes were disbanded, freeing the lease system from the continuation of such interferences and restraints).

THE COOPERATIVE SECTOR

By contrast, the final Law on Cooperatives provides a market-type environment for movement of resources in cooperative activity. Equipment, labor services, and the necessary space can be bought, financed with bank credits if necessary, and collectively owned. The sector can offer substantial opportunities for absorbing labor that the planners expect to release from industry. Many would find lucrative opportunities for making a ruble under more or less independent working conditions. The risk takers, among them skilled workers, engineers, and middle-level managers, may decide to form challenging ventures and finally escape the boredom of state jobs. The negative impact of an expanding light manufacturing and service sector on foreign exchange earnings would be minimal. Consumers would find a vast array of services and items for which there is a pent-up demand.

Currently there are about twenty thousand cooperatives, which employ one-half of 1 percent of the labor force. The reverberating success stories are the Moscow restaurants and the taxi services. How far and how fast cooperative activity will expand beyond these activities will depend not only on the alacrity with which enterprising citizens avail themselves of the opportunities but also on the speed with which the rest of the economy is freed. Potential cooperative ventures in manufacturing and processing activities will not materialize if shortages and irregular supplies continue plaguing Soviet industry in general.

FOREIGN TRADE

The failure of the reformers to take the necessary big leap in conceptualizing the new order is manifest also in the area of foreign trade.

As I remarked earlier, exports and their destinations in the traditional Soviet arrangement are set by the FTOS rather than by the producers. Imports and their sources are also decided by the FTOS, rather than the using enterprises. By contrast, foreign trade decisions in market economies are taken autonomously by a myriad of economic agents, which results in balance of trade and payment surpluses and deficits. Exchange rates are then adjusted as a way of reconciling the resulting foreign exchange supplies and demands.

The Soviet reforms currently in place do not conform to this model of foreign trade. The flexibility and autonomy in matters of foreign trade introduced for a few enterprises amount therefore to tinkering rather than reform. The trade turnover handled by ministries (through their FTOS) and enterprises had increased roughly to 20 percent by the beginning of 1988 (Hewett 1988b, 4). It is difficult, however, to assess the amount of this modest turnover that was handled by the enterprises rather than the FTOs in the ministries. Convincing evidence that the planners have moved away from the early authoritarianism of the FTO "nanny" (in the Ministry of Foreign Trade) to independent decision making by individual enterprises is still missing.

Moreover, the planners have not managed to shake off the traditional practice of linking the import liability of a foreign transaction with its potential export earnings. The notion that exports and imports can and should be undertaken by independent actors for gains from trade to be at their maximum is absent. Hence the near total insistence on linking the import liabilities of a joint venture with its own export earnings. This "closed-loop" approach to foreign exchange transactions at the intra-enterprise level is an exception rather than the rule in market economies. Unless this constraint is softened, the recent announcement that foreign companies will be allowed majority ownership in joint ventures will not attract substantial investments from abroad.

While the reforms appear to be a big step forward, they are a modest departure. They make sense only if they are the first step toward a necessary and more systemic reorganization of the foreign trade regime.

Changing the "Superstructure": Beyond Economic Reforms

IF THE capitalist markets are kept at bay in the design of perestroika, so also is the capitalist political system. There is no mincing of words here. The country will march forward under the guidance of the Communist Party on the basis of Lenin's precepts. The Western political system, with its separation of powers, multiparty system and elections, free press, and independent judiciary, currently has no place in the reforms.

But the existing political arrangements cannot continue. As with economic restructuring, the challenges of reforming current Soviet "politics" are formidable. The proposed changes nevertheless reveal Mikhail Gorbachev's view of the exercise of political power and his objectives.

What is Gorbachev's view of power? He is a Communist and a true believer, and the monopoly of the Communist Party in the political life of the land is an article of faith that he will not give up easily. Besides, it would be a grave mistake to do so. It would unleash uncontrollable forces that could dislodge him and jeopardize even the modest elements in his program. At the same time, increased participation by the people at various levels is necessary, in Gorbachev's view, for ensuring the success of the economic reforms. Where should the line between political control and permissiveness be drawn? That is the issue.

In Stalin's view of the exercise of power, this question was absent. He was not only authoritarian but cruel. The novelist Chingiz Aitmatov recounts a story in which Stalin revealed this streak in full measure. Stalin demanded, "Bring me a chicken and I will show you how to rule the people." He plucked its feathers to its pink skin and scattered a handful of grain on the ground, whereupon the bird followed him everywhere. "This is the way to rule the people," he is reported to have said.

By contrast, Gorbachev's notion of wielding power is subtle and, certainly, more humane. Several incidents at the June Party Conference brought this out vividly.

A Stavropol delegate at the Conference addressed him directly and suggested that those who are opposed to restructuring should be "driven out . . . pensioned off." The delegate continued, "I am sure the Conference will give you and the Politburo the necessary authority" (*Pravda*, July 1, 1988). Gorbachev interrupted him: "Let us discuss this issue in the presence of witnesses. You have presented Mikhail Sergeevich [Gorbachev] as being too simple. If we once again start with the Central Committee removing people working with you in Stavropol or elsewhere, or a bit higher, in the Russian Federation or anywhere else, it won't work. That has happened before in the country. A lot of things were done from above. Nothing comes out of this" (*Pravda*, July 1, 1988). Yet another delegate spoke without mincing words. "Mikhail Sergeevich," he said, "you have to bang your fist" (*Pravda*, July 1, 1988). Gorbachev's response was equally forthright: "If that is what you want, then let us start banging. . . . As for banging and as for the fist, it has been pretty much perfected in our country. . . . As we begin resolving the tasks of renewing the party and society, we must refrain from using old methods that we want to give up and that brought our country to this plight" (*Pravda*, July 1, 1988). Then there was the actor Mikhail Ulyanov, who made an impassioned plea for creating legal guarantees that would prevent "an evil person" from "issuing orders, intimidating people, and letting blood. . . . And the fact that this is a real possibility is shown by the bitter and frightening

FIGS. 6.1. and 6.2. The boredom at a 1983 Central Committee meeting on the faces of, right to left, Mikhail Gorbachev, Viktor Grishin, and Nikolai Tikhonov (top)—the latter two subsequently retired—contrasts tellingly with the evident animation of General Secretary Gorbachev at the June 1988 Party Conference (bottom) as he argues with Aleksandr Yakovlev while Yegor Ligachev looks on. Since then, Yakovlev has been "moved up" to head a commission in charge of international affairs and Ligachev has been "moved down" to handle agriculture. Reuters/Bettmann newsphotos.

article of Nina Andreeva.* This took us quite by surprise. Many, if not all, of us stood to attention and waited for our next instructions" (*Pravda*, June 30, 1988). How did Gorbachev respond to Ulyanov's implied suggestion that communications intimidating the supporters of perestroika should be suppressed? He was not going to be caught off guard with respect to the Andreeva letter, which had silenced the media for almost three weeks in the spring of 1988. While Ligachev listened, he said: "She has sent a communication. We have just received it. It has been passed on to the members of the Presidium who will read it. She insists that she is right" (*Pravda*, June 30, 1988).

These encounters certainly do not reveal Gorbachev as a Jeffersonian democrat leading a chorus of "we, the people." Rather, they are marked by a mixture of candor, tactical maneuvering, and a desire to curtail arbitrariness in the exercise of power. All viewpoints must be presented, debated, and sorted out by widespread participation. The opponents of perestroika must be heard too. They should not be purged from the top or silenced with the banging of fists.

But Gorbachev has no intention of allowing them to prevail. At the very least, they must be identified. The party functionaries who meddle in local administration, who issue orders to collective farms against the farms' better judgment and interfere in the routine activities of state enterprises, must be restrained and preferably removed by democratic procedures. Of course, the resistance to economic reform comes also from workers who feel threatened by loss of jobs, and the people at large who fail to

---

* The letter, signed by a Leningrad professor named Nina Andreeva but presumably inspired by Ligachev, appeared in *Sovetskaia rossiia* in March 1988. It was essentially a neo-Stalinist document and contained an ideological and political attack on the Gorbachev program. It was described as "the political manifesto of the anti-perestroika forces" in the reply, supposedly written by Aleksandr Yakovlev, that appeared in *Pravda* three weeks later,

experience improvements in their living standards. These groups, however, have to be won over by a careful unfolding of the reform strategy and concrete results. Gorbachev believes that at every stage it is important to implement the strategy so that some gains are visible. Here, the party functionaries and their meddlesome ways are the obstacle. But they can be made to behave if they are threatened with loss of power by giving the voters a choice to elect others. The first business of the day, therefore, is to change the procedures for election of individuals to the party and the government at all levels. (Current election procedures are described in Appendix 2.)

Gorbachev's views of political power and the proposed political reforms for fulfilling perestroika have to be compatible with the monopoly of the Communist Party. And indeed they are, as I argue below. But something more must be ensured in the process of political restructuring. The reforms must be designed to promote Gorbachev's continuing survival as the leader of the party. Perestroika must advance under his guidance. The natural instinct of a politician is self-preservation, and Gorbachev has not made his way to the top to watch his self-destruction. The consolidation of power in his hands, at the same time, must result from legitimate means and be achieved in deliberate steps. The current practice whereby the General Secretary is chosen and can be removed by a handful of men in the Politburo (with or without the approval of the Central Committee) is not only arbitrary but risky. At the June Party Conference, he proposed a switch to a presidential form of government in which the President, with broad powers in domestic and foreign affairs, is to be elected by a much larger Congress of People's Deputies. While there is safety in numbers, Gorbachev must feel reasonably confident of his leadership and his program to suggest the change. (Gorbachev preferred the term "President." The Conference delegates opted for the title "Chairman.")

REFORM IN POLITICS

The proposed changes in the political arrangements were initiated formally in May 1988 when the Central Committee adopted several "theses" subsequently approved by the June Party Conference.

The issue that the Central Committee wrestled with was the restoration of inner-party democracy within a single-party system. How could party committees, at all levels, be prevented from acting arbitrarily and meddling in the activities of local administrations (soviets) and enterprises? The proposed changes focused on the role of party functionaries and the procedures for electing them.

It was decided that all party officials, starting at the district and city levels, should be limited to two consecutive five-year terms with the possibility of a third term if it is approved by no less than 75 percent of the membership of the relevant party organization. More than one candidate could contest an election, which would be by secret ballot. The tenure limitation would apply to members of the Politburo, the party Secretariat, and the General Secretary himself.

As for the constraints on the role of party officials, they were rather in the nature of attempts at converting a predatory carnivore to self-denying vegetarianism. The officials were asked to refrain from meddling in the activities of the local soviets and enterprises. They should guide and inspire, they were told, rather than interfere and supersede. Perhaps, faced with the prospect of contested elections, limited tenure, and exhortations to forsake the exercise of power, they might turn to other activities.

These proposals were debated at the June Party Conference. So also was Gorbachev's suggestion of a tricameral Congress of People's Deputies with the power to elect a President with genuine authority in domestic and foreign affairs. The third chamber of the Congress would consist of representatives to be elected from the professions, the arts, the media, and the like. The supporters of perestroika could be expected to belong to these groups.

Whether these reforms would suffice to effectively separate "government" at all levels from party control, as in Western models of separation of powers, was a matter of considerable debate at the June Party Conference. In particular, the arrangements Gorbachev has inherited (as described in Appendix 2) ensure the domination of the party committee and its secretary over the executive committees of the soviets at all levels. The party secretary is invariably a member of the executive committee, if not its chairman. He usually gets elected to the soviet (and subsequently by the soviet to the executive committee) because he has the weight of the party and its resources at his command, and the elections are uncontested. Now, with many candidates and a secret ballot, he could lose the election. Would he, and with him the party committee, then gracefully withdraw into a noninterfering mode? Gorbachev's response was cryptic: "You can draw the appropriate conclusion," he was reported to have said. What did he have in mind? Having lost the election, the party secretary obviously could not be on the executive committee. With his credibility damaged at the ballot box, he might even be maneuvered out of the party leadership under the best-case scenario. But events might turn out to be less fortunate. The skeptics were worried even more about the alternative possibility—a victory of a party secretary in an election to a soviet. Surely party control over administration could hardly cease in that event. A more critical question was posed by the economist Abalkin: Can a one-party system be truly democratized without an explicit recognition of the principle of a legal opposition? In his response (*Pravda*, July 1, 1988), Gorbachev evaded the issue, suggesting rhetorically that his economic adviser lacked faith in the Communist system.

Notwithstanding the doubts and the debates, the proposals for political reform were approved by the Conference. Their actual implementation will stretch over the next several months, requiring formal acceptance at appropriate levels. The Central Committee of the party has already approved the proposal of the Politburo to set up a commission, with Gorbachev as the chairman, to supervise the implementation of the reforms. Gorbachev's timetable is expeditious. The proposed changes in the election procedures are to be codified in a new Constitution by the end of November so that the Congress of People's Deputies and the Supreme Soviet can be elected, according to the new rules, in March 1989.

In the meantime, elections with multiple candidates, by secret ballot, were held in September 1988 to fill party positions at the lowest levels—400,000 in all. About a third of the leaders elected in the initial 30,000 party units were new, compared to a fifth in 1987 (*New York Times*, September 21, 1988). There were signs that the old guard was being dislodged. But perhaps not with the speed to fit Gorbachev's schedule, and certainly not at the top of the hierarchy. In an electrifying move at the end of the month, Gorbachev called a session of the Central Committee and of the Supreme Soviet. The Committee voted to streamline the party apparatus at the top by eliminating some and consolidating the rest of the twenty-two departments in the party Secretariat and appointing six commissions to provide policy guidelines in key areas. The Supreme Soviet accepted the resignation (already approved by the Central Committee) of Andrei Gromyko as President and elected Gorbachev to succeed him. Technically, Gorbachev will remain the ceremonial chairman of the Supreme Soviet until he is elected President under the new provisions accepted by the party Conference for inclusion in the Soviet Constitution. (I will discuss the relevance of the personnel changes at the top for Gorbachev's survival in chapter 9.)

Several questions are prompted by these proposed changes and their systematic implementation. Will the Soviet Union evolve into a democracy? In particular, will the changes pave the way for fulfilling the various demands of the ethnic minorities? Will there be better prospects of gains from the economic reforms?

The General Secretary does not intend the changes to result in a Western-style democracy. He has cautioned that the unfolding democracy should not be used for "undemocratic" purposes such as redrawing ethnic boundaries or setting up new political parties. However, active discussion of local affairs and greater participation in the workplace will emerge. Moreover, with increased tolerance and legal guarantees (which I discuss below), people will enjoy a modicum of civil liberties. Ownership of personal belongings will be protected by law. Diversity of religious beliefs and cultural freedoms will be on the rise. Routine censoring of letters and telephones will decline. Choices in careers will open up. However, institutionalized dissent on matters of foreign policy, military decisions, and superpower status is certainly not on the agenda, now or in the near future. Euphoria on this front is therefore uncalled for.

What would be the impact of the proposed political changes on fulfilling ethnic aspirations? These demands have escalated into violent clashes between Christian Armenians and Moslem Azerbaijanis. The former insist that the small enclave of Nagorno-Karabakh, which is located in the Republic of Azerbaijan and has a majority of Armenians, should be transferred to Armenia. Then there are the demands for greater political and economic autonomy by the populations of the Baltic republics of Estonia, Latvia, and Lithuania, which were annexed to Soviet territory in 1940 on the basis of a secret protocol to the nonaggression treaty of 1939 between the Soviet Union and Nazi Germany. Finally, the Crimean Tartars, who were exiled to Uzbekistan during World War II because their loyalty was under suspicion, have been demonstrating to return to their homeland in the Crimea.

The final official decision on Nagorno-Karabakh (*Pravda*, July 20, 1988) ruled out the transfer of the enclave (although its legislature had voted to become part of Armenia) because the Azerbaijani legislature had voted against it. Article 78 of the Soviet Constitution requires that the republics involved in a boundary dispute should agree to a redrawing of boundaries. If the demands for secession persist, resulting in violence and subversive activity, they will undoubtedly be put down with harsh measures.

Short of changing territorial boundaries, Gorbachev is inclined to consider demands for increased political and economic autonomy, especially if a concession wins him support for perestroika. This give-and-take is evident with regard to the Baltic republics. The opposition fronts in the republics, while demanding greater autonomy from central control, have a pro-perestroika slant, and Communist Party members as their leaders. Their flourishing economies can supply consumer goods and livestock products, and so contribute to the fight against shortages. The Baltic populations were allowed to demonstrate against the Nazi-Soviet pact on its anniversary in late August 1988. Of course this benign, positive-sum arrangement between the center and the republics would disappear if their demands were to step beyond the permissible limits. Over the long haul, however, political perestroika has the potential for benefiting Soviet nationalities in general by allowing them greater freedom for cultural identity, more educational opportunities, and upward mobility into better jobs vis-à-vis the Russians.

Finally, what would be the impact of these political reforms on the gains from economic reforms? Many, aided by Gorbachev's occasional pronouncements, have suggested that the political reforms will produce substantial economic gains. Certainly, as I argued in chapter 5, some static gains in efficiency will result if party functionaries are retired or stop meddling in enterprise and farm affairs. But surely the large dynamic gains depend on enterprise and farm freedom to innovate, invest, produce, and sell in a market environment. These freedoms are certainly not contemplated under the current program, which seriously limits the scope of economic gains that can be expected from the political reforms.*

It is necessary to remember also that political changes in the direction of democratization are not necessarily helpful on the economic front (although the American liberal tradition does tend to accept the Panglossian view that "all good things go together"). And there are unfortunate examples, as in Pinochet's Chile, where regression on the political front has been associated with comparative economic success, and fortunate examples such as Deng Xiaoping's China, where near-atrophy on political reform has coexisted with major economic gains from a substantial restructuring of the economic framework. (I discuss this contrast with the Soviet situation in chapter 8.)

Let me then turn to changes in the "superstructure" outside of politics. These changes on the current Soviet scene are truly far-reaching. There are momentous strides in the arts, literature, and the media. The eradication of the imprint of Stalinism from Soviet history and culture, from the past and the present, is the purpose and the challenge. Then there are the proposed reforms in law and education. Where is this engine of change heading?

PERESTROIKA IN CULTURE AND HISTORY

There can be no perestroika in culture and history without lifting the oppressive burden of Stalinism from Soviet life. This has been the critical item on Gorbachev's agenda, and a problematic one. In discussing it, a backward glance is necessary.

The first giant step was taken by Khrushchev in 1956 at the Twentieth Party Congress when he denounced Stalin and his crimes in a "secret" speech. Millions of prisoners were released from Stalinist camps and restored to civilian life. At no other time, in no other place, did so many find

---

* That the political reforms are nonetheless part of a coherent strategy for economic reforms, aside from being an end in themselves, is discussed in chapter 8.

freedom and dignity as a result of a single initiative, which Solzhenitsyn described as a "movement of the heart." Four years were to pass before the next assault, again at Khrushchev's initiative, on Stalin's cult. Not only was the sarcophagus in Red Square containing his body removed, but other physical traces of his memory were eradicated. Except in Georgia, hundreds of towns and cities, streets and squares, factories and farms, were given new names, and all monuments to the dictator were removed.

Stalin has proven difficult to dislodge, however. Within months of his "secret" speech, Khrushchev was "obliged to declare in a number of speeches that Stalin 'was a great Marxist-Leninist' and 'a great revolutionary' and that the party 'would not allow Stalin's name to be surrendered to the enemies of Communism.' He also sharply condemned the concept of 'Stalinism', which he alleged to be an invention of anti-Soviet propaganda" (Medvedev 1983, 96). Four years later, the second time around, Khrushchev resisted the "strident demands" to punish everyone connected with the repressive measures of the thirties and to rehabilitate the victims of the 1936–1938 trials. The process stopped short of rehabilitating some of the prominent figures, among them Bukharin, Kamenev, and Zinoviev.

There were also new stirrings under Khrushchev in the cultural life of the country. As in politics, they were to be short-lived although filled with consequential and colorful events. The battle lines were drawn between the "liberals," led by the poets Tvardovsky and Yevtushenko and the sculptor Ernst Neizvestny, and the "conservatives" poised to squash the fresh start. In the center was Khrushchev himself in the role of the supreme arbiter ready to ventilate his views on literature, painting, and sculpture. Here, he was a committed Communist: just as Stalin's crimes were to be denounced because they deviated from the principles of communism, works of art and literature that did not conform to socialist realism and serve the people were to be proscribed. His approval of the publication of *One Day in the Life of Ivan Denisovitch* in *Novyi Mir*, a decision in which he carried the Presidium of the Central Committee, was in line with this argument. This was great literature but an even greater exposé of the Stalinist camps. His reaction to the abstract works in the exhibition of contemporary art in Moscow was predictable, too. "A donkey could do better with its tail," he was reported to have said to Neizvestny. He offered his credentials as an art critic in the following words: " 'When I was a miner, I didn't understand. When I was a junior Party official, I didn't understand. At every level on my way up the ladder, I didn't understand. Today I am premier and leader of the Party: surely I'm able to understand things now, aren't I?' " (Medvedev 1983, 218). Yevtushenko's plea that certain "formalist tendencies" in the work of abstract artists "will be straightened out in time" met with a decisive retort from Khrushchev: " 'The grave straightens out the hunchback' " (Medvedev 1983, 219). His ideological opposition to abstract art and formalist music continued until the end of his leadership. He made another "astonishing volte face," praising Stalin's services to the party and the world Communist movement and his "devotion" to Marxism and communism. The treatment of Stalinist repression in contemporary literature was a "dangerous topic," and the "material difficult to handle" (Medvedev 1983, 220). The curtain was finally drawn on works dealing with the topic by a formal ban.

It was therefore not surprising that Soviet culture during the succeeding Brezhnev era was a wasteland. Stalinist terror was a forbidden subject and culture was called upon to serve the good of the cause. Those who dared break official sanctions did so clandestinely. When the writer Vladimir Voinovich was asked to reveal the secret of his creative writing, he was reported to have said: "I write one page and then I hide it. I write another page and then I hide it."

The principal lesson Gorbachev appears to have drawn from these "liberalization" swings under Khrushchev is that attacking Stalin is a risky business because it amounts to attacking socialism, the world Communist movement, the legitimacy of the party, and the fair name of the motherland by digging up a murky past. The strategy cannot be as black-or-white as banishing Stalin and Stalinism and bringing in perestroika. Gorbachev therefore deliberately adopted a middle-of-the-road pitch at the celebration marking the seventieth anniversary of the Revolution: Stalin's contributions in building the economy and leading the country during the war were acknowledged, but the cult was rejected as antisocialist and antidemocratic. He gave the devil his due but made clear that there could be no place for the Stalinist cult in perestroika.

But formal acceptance by the party of this version of de-Stalinization came only with the June Party Conference. In the meantime Stalin surfaced once more in the antiperestroika manifesto (*Sovietskaia rossiia*, March 13, 1988, 3), signed by Nina Andreeva but sponsored by Ligachev. She even cited Churchill's endorsement of the great dictator: "He was a man with an impressive personality and . . . exceptional energy, . . . unyielding and merciless in action and words which even I, reared in the British Parliament, was at a loss to counter. He found Russia with a wooden plough but left it with atomic weapons." The endorsement of de-Stalinization became particularly graphic when the Party Conference approved the resolution to create a monument to Stalin's victims. What greater reward could have come the way of the human-rights activist Andrei Sakharov, the historian Roy Medvedev, and the poet Yevgeny Yevtushenko than to be part of the committee entrusted with the task of organizing the memorial?

In the meantime, the creative energies of the country have started flowing in tumultuous celebration. In literature and films, the treatment of the theme of Stalin's terror has gone beyond the gulag to bigger challenges. One can now ask: Was Stalin Lenin's heir? Two plays by Shatrov— *The Brest Peace* and *Onward, Onward, Onward*—wrestle with this theme using Lenin, Stalin, Bukharin, Trotsky, and lesser characters to re-create those exciting, agonizing, days. Can the pervasive traces of Stalinism be erased? The film *Repentance*, which played to packed audiences, has a plot twist in which the dictator's dead body comes back to life. Weren't there traces of Hitler's tyranny during the terror under Stalin? Vasily Grossman's monumental novel *Life and Fate*, currently being serialized in *Oktiabr'*, deals with this formidable theme. The literati are certainly ahead of the historians in filling some of the "blank pages." Does it really matter if some details are slightly inaccurate?

But can literature and the arts deviate from the crushing theme of socialist realism and Marxist orthodoxy? If Pasternak and Bulgakov are in, can Nabokov and Solzhenitsyn be far behind? The *Cancer Ward* can be published but not the rest of Solzhenitsyn's manifestly anti-Communist works. Right now, Nabokov's prospects are dim; his *Lolita* has too sizzling a sexual theme and his émigré novel *The Gift* is too irreverent toward Nikolai Chernyshevsky, the torchbearer of Marxist thought.

While the restrictions on the creative imagination have become less severe, the media have become venturesome. Newspapers, magazines, and television have become interesting, even entertaining, and they more accurately reflect real life. The ban has been lifted from reporting on alcoholism, crime, drug abuse, prostitution, homosexuality, the crumbling health-care system, plane crashes (including a rare hijacking), and accidents in general. On this side of the Atlantic the Beatles have been retired, but on Soviet morning TV they are thriving. The viewer can also exercise to the beat of socialist aerobics. The evening news is followed by "Spotlight on Perestroika," in which reporters quiz factory managers and local officials with the incisive persistence of Sam Donaldson. The grand political spectacle on television was the June Party Conference. Delegates argued and debated, and voted both for and against resolutions; a delegate denounced "people who in earlier days actively supported the policy of stagnation" and, encouraged by Gorbachev, named Andrei Gromyko,

Mikhail Solomentsev (a Politburo member, now retired), Viktor Afanasyev (*Pravda* editor), and Georgii Arbatov (foreign policy adviser) as men "unfit to remain in the Party or Soviet organs"; Boris El'tsin pleaded for his reha- bilitation and Ligachev ridiculed him as a "destructive force." Never in recent memory has there been such an opportunity to watch history in the making.

Can the cultural thaw and the seemingly free exchange of views in print and on television lead to the emergence of political pluralism? Political pluralism starts with the creation of institutionalized groups, including caucuses and lobbies, that profess a stand on a given issue and perhaps put out a manifesto. From all current indications, such activism is to be allowed selectively. For starters, the publishing and programming monopoly still rests with the state: the Law on Cooperatives does not include the pub- lishing and printing of books, magazines, and newspapers among the permissible activities of cooperatives. The ex- plorations in history, the themes of ferment in literature and the cinema, the debates on economic and social issues in the media, probe the limits but are carefully navigated. The function of glasnost' is to arouse the populace from apathy and encourage political activism within limits that extend only as far as reforming communism rather than replacing it with an alternative regime.

From this perspective, Roy Medvedev and Andrei Sa- kharov are reformers whose political agenda has been, more or less, co-opted by perestroika, whereas the sociolo- gist Zaslavskaya's call (*Pravda*, May 24, 1988) for the forma- tion of a "non-Communist alliance of unofficial groups and individuals" appears to push perestroika beyond these bounds with bolder proposals for political and social change. An example of acceptable activism is the forma- tion, with official blessings, of the non-Communist fronts in the Baltic republics for promoting greater political and economic independence for these republics. At the fringe is the Democratic Union, founded by the activist Sergei Grigoryants for the declared purpose of doing away with the Communist state. Grigoryants was promptly dispatched to prison to serve a one-week sentence.

THE PROPOSED REFORMS IN LAW

Soviet legal reform under Mikhail Gorbachev has two dimensions. Because the state owns and manages almost everything, it needs a supporting structure of laws to carry out its activities. Perestroika of the economy has therefore required continuing legislation. The other dimension, which is considered here, is the relationship between law and the citizen in a Communist state.

A critical feature of the system is that the citizens enjoy as much freedom and as many rights as the state decides to give them. The participants in the lively debates that have arisen with the advent of glasnost' have therefore focused on two aspects: first, that Soviet law is antiquated and, second, that the intention of the law should be effectively carried out. In other words, law should be humanized by increased "decriminalization," and the actual implementation of laws should be improved.

As is to be expected, the concept of legal defense and the status of the law courts are different in the Soviet Union from their Western counterparts. "Innocent until proven guilty" implies that one cannot be imprisoned simply by being charged with an offense. And one is entitled to a defense lawyer immediately. In the Soviet Union, by contrast, "guilty unless proven innocent" tends to be the legal precept. There are no Miranda rights, pretrial detention is the practice, and the often ill-trained and underpaid defense lawyers appear after the preliminary investigation is completed.

More to the point, the courts are not independent. They bear the heavy burden of "our own experience" (Gorbachev 1987, 105). They must battle with the leftover legacy of Stalinist arbitrariness and of pervasive "lawlessness" under Brezhnev. In particular, the heavy hand of the party in the execution of laws and in the function of law courts persists. As for the concept of punishment, it is quite often disproportionate to the nature of the crime. One cannot truly grasp the notion of "cruel and unusual" punishment unless one is exiled to Siberia, or, in recent times, confined in a psychiatric ward, or hauled up before a firing squad for more serious crimes.

Legal reform, therefore, has focused on some of these issues. In a recent interview (*Pravda*, December 5, 1987), the chairman of the Soviet Supreme Court, Judge Vladimir Terebilov, suggested several changes—among them, instituting proper defense procedures, reducing pretrial detention, abolishing internal exile, and reducing punishment for lesser crimes.

A significant step, beginning on January 1, 1988, was taken by the Supreme Soviet when it endorsed legal procedures enabling individuals to employ Article 58 of the Soviet Constitution, which states that the "actions of officials committed in violation of the law, in excess of their powers, and impinging upon the rights of citizens" may be appealed in a court (Butler 1988, 5). The need for admitting a defense counsel in preliminary investigations of criminal cases was acknowledged in a decree of the Central Committee, dated November 30, 1986. The June Party Conference carried the reform further by endorsing the doctrine of presumption of innocence. The delegates recognized the need for continuous revision of the law in the interest of social change. They endorsed the proposal that everything that is explicitly not prohibited is permitted.

In which areas will these prohibitions continue? State security and press censorship are the obvious candidates. Article 70 of the Soviet Constitution relating to "anti-Soviet agitation and propaganda" and Article 190-1 prohibiting the "circulation of fabrications known to be false that defame the Soviet state and social system" will remain in place, although their scope may be narrowed. The KGB will continue being vigilant, but it will be more selective, less arbitrary, and increasingly less secretive. In a recent interview (*Pravda*, August 29, 1988) the former head of the KGB,

Viktor Chebrikov, said that while information would increasingly be declassified, the process should not be construed as implying "lack of vigilance and effort at safeguarding state secrets."

PROPOSED REFORMS IN EDUCATION

Finally, there are proposals to reform the educational system. As can be imagined, these are not designed to promote free thought but to remove excessive regimentation, loosen central control, and provide the schools with adequate physical equipment.

The regimentation is reflected in the way education is imparted. The two million teachers instruct close to forty million elementary and secondary students in about 129,000 schools from the same textbooks and curriculum under the watchful eyes of the Ministry of Education and the Academy of Pedagogical Sciences. The curriculum is so detailed as to leave little scope for innovation. Ivan can read, write, and add, but he tends to become bored and even alienated. Excessive centralization arises from the implicit enforcement of career choices on students from the age of around fifteen, when they are directed into a specific educational stream with entry into vocational schools or universities. Whether one becomes a lathe operator or a surgeon is more or less decided at that time.

The primitive conditions of the schools were laid bare by no less a person than Yegor Ligachev in a speech (*Pravda*, February 18, 1988) to the Central Committee containing a flurry of statistics: 21 percent of the schools had no central heating, 30 percent lacked running water, and 40 percent had no indoor toilets. National investment in education had declined from 11 percent of the budget in 1970 to 8 percent in 1986.

Secretary General Gorbachev plans to reform this system and to reduce the alienation and apathy that it breeds. Even the conservative Ligachev argued in his Central Committee speech for less "primitive standardization" and more variety in teaching methods. Economists should note his suggestion that economics instruction should emphasize the role of profits and incentives, though it is to be schizophrenically within the constraint of socialist ideology and hence handicapped at the start. But the proposed reform is nevertheless important and can push Soviet education in the direction of less regimentation and greater vitality. Ligachev's remark that the ideological monitoring of schools by local bureaucrats is to be softened by local councils of teachers, parents, and industry representatives could produce local activism in educational matters.

Adding to the doctrinal and conformist pressures on the young is the presence of the Komsomol—the youth wing of the Communist Party. The current membership is around thirty-eight million, down by four million since 1985. Evidently, the young find its activities doctrinaire and boring. Recently, its monopoly has been threatened by several informal groups espousing social, political, and ecological causes. *Komsomolskaia pravda* (January 31, 1988) reacted to the phenomenon with a vitriolic attack on the credentials of the group leaders. Given long-standing Soviet practices, these attacks go beyond the verbal and degenerate into physical intimidation, denial of admission to a school, demotion from a job, and other punitive acts. "Socialist competition" in the political arena, for now at least, is fraught with danger for the newcomers. But the mere fact that the hegemony of the Komsomol is challenged by the young is a refreshing signal.

What do all these changes in politics, in literature and the arts, the media, law, and education amount to? Is the old order giving way to a new sociopolitical system? Several surviving features of the old order are outdated and distorted. At the top of the list are the Stalinist vestiges, subtle and oppressive, of the Brezhnev years. Gorbachev's purpose has been to clean out these remnants and encourage dialogue within limits that are clearly defined. The supremacy of the Communist Party is to be supported by a bureaucratic apparatus that will be substantially streamlined and continually renovated. The media will be freer, the judiciary will be less arbitrary, and the educational system will be less regimented.

Gorbachev insists on describing the arrangement as "socialist democracy." It is certainly different from democratic socialism. According to a Polish wit, they are as far apart as an electric chair from an ordinary chair. But I would not go that far. As a result of these changes, people are being allowed a longer leash to roam around, to express views and ask questions. Over time, Soviet society should evolve, albeit slowly, into a lively and vigorous arena, somewhat like Hungary or Poland, in which the bureaucrats have dwindled in numbers and importance, the media have become more daring, the judiciary insists on protecting the permissible rights of the citizens, and the youth, above all, have become increasingly irrepressible.

Foreign Policy: New Thinking and Initiatives

MATCHING THE SPEED with which Mikhail Gorbachev has moved on the broader, noneconomic aspects of reform is the rapidity with which Soviet foreign policy has been recast by him. Old policies and ideological attitudes in regard to the three traditional areas of Soviet interest—Eastern Europe, the Third World, and the United States—are now in unparalleled flux. Once again, the motivation seems twofold: to reexamine the old practices in a search for better, more efficient, ways of achieving given political goals and to seek indirect economic benefits that will aid the new efforts at economic restructuring.

FOREIGN POLICY: OBJECTIVES AND PROBLEMS

At the end of World War II in 1945, the Soviet Union, exhausted from the war, was in disarray, its economy in ruins. By the time Gorbachev became General Secretary nearly four decades later, the Soviet Union ranked as a superpower with a formidable military arsenal. But the economic situation he inherited was no less dismaying, whereas the resources expended in carrying out new responsibilities—in managing the restive Eastern European partners, in underwriting interventions and interests in the Third World, and, above all, in engaging in an unceasing arms race with the United States—were enormous and crippling.

The combination of military overstretch and economic weakness and its inescapable consequences were evident. As with the reform of the economy and political arrangements, the rethinking of history, and glasnost' in culture, Mikhail Gorbachev had to undertake a bold and fresh assessment of the role of foreign policy and the military buildup in the current predicament. Some of his initiatives have already produced positive results.

The challenges of the foreign policy agenda to the Soviet leadership have traditionally come from various directions. The "imperialist threat" from the United States had to be countered with an appropriate response in the shape of a military buildup, diplomatic initiatives, and ideological rhetoric. Maintaining the stability of the Soviet bloc in Eastern Europe through the continued presence of Soviet troops and the occasional rolling of Soviet tanks has been an essential ingredient of the strategy of ensuring territorial security and holding "imperialism" at bay. The conflict with China, marked by ideological vehemence and border clashes in the early years, has also had to be handled in the context of the superpower equation. The Soviet role in the Third World, economic at first and increasingly military later, has again reflected superpower rivalry.

In none of these areas have Gorbachev's predecessors had a tranquil life. There have been dramatic reverses, such as the expulsion from Egypt, the fiasco in Afghanistan, and the "loss of China" to the United States. There have been modest failures, such as the waning Soviet influence in the Third World. There have also been sources of growing worry, such as restive Eastern Europe. And looming above it all has been the arms race with the United States, exacting its toll on the U.S. economy through the budget deficit, and debilitating the Soviet Union through a massive absorption of scarce resources by the military establishment.

Quiet reflection on these problems and the inefficacy of past methods of addressing them, along with their consequences for the Soviet economy and for the prospects of perestroika, has prompted Gorbachev and his advisers to a serious reexamination of the conduct of foreign policy and to a search for new initiatives.

NEW THINKING

The reexamination of past methods is manifest in several recent, forthright critiques by influential analysts. They focus on undue emphasis on "military" rather than "political" responses to security threats and objectives—a theme not unfamiliar on this side of the street. They refer to ideological overreach evident in the "hegemonic" effort to establish Communist systems elsewhere. They deplore "narrowly elitist" decision-making processes that reinforce, rather than contain, these errors.

The critics include the prominent historian Vyacheslav Dashichev (*Literaturnaia gazeta*, May 18, 1988, 14). He went so far as to suggest that Soviet foreign policy under Stalin, driven by "hegemonism," may itself have prompted the "imperialist centers of power" to react with an arms build-up backed by the legitimate notions of "containment" and "deterrence." Dashichev thus implied that George Kennan (1947, 566–82) had been right when he described Soviet expansionism as "a fluid stream which moves constantly, wherever it is permitted to move . . . [until] . . . it has filled every nook and cranny available to it in the basin of economic power." As a result of "hegemonism," the Soviet Union was perceived as a dangerous power bent on destroying bourgeois democracies and setting up Soviet-style Communist regimes around the world. And it provoked a corresponding response.

Dashichev also argued that, even when the objectives were peaceful, such as security, disarmament, and cooperation under Brezhnev, the solutions and methods had been military rather than political. Equally unfortunate, the "narrowly elitist" formulation of policy had resulted in the misuse of the opportunity furnished by détente. Instead of using this new phase in international relations to usher in economic improvement and democratization at home, Soviet policymakers had squandered the opportunity. The West had concluded in consequence that détente had been used by the Soviet leadership to build its military forces in an attempt to gain parity with the West.

Again, the prominent journalist Aleksandr Bovin (*Izvestiia*, June 16, 1988) wrote emphatically: "In my view, the deployment of SS-20 missiles in Europe and the introduction of troops in Afghanistan were typical examples of the subjective decisions based on the desire to use military force in foreign policy." The growing chorus against knee-jerk militarism in foreign policy was joined by the formidable Oleg Bogomolov, director of Moscow's prestigious Institute of the World Socialist System. Writing in *Literaturnaia gazeta* (March 16, 1988, 10), he revealed that within weeks of the invasion of Afghanistan, an Institute memorandum had predicted that the invasion would result in unleashing the combined opposition of the United States, NATO, China, the Muslim world, and, most definitely, the "rebel army of the Afghan feudal-clerical circles." Other negative consequences had been laid out, too: it would end détente, damage Soviet prestige in the nonaligned movement and the Islamic world, and doom the prospects of improving relations with China. The unerring analysis and the prophetic scenario had gone unheeded.

But the most dramatic critic of foreign policy remained Mikhail Gorbachev himself. Speaking at the June Party Conference (*Pravda*, June 29, 1988), he addressed eloquently the theme of foreign policy formulation—its style, content, and consequences. Decisions had been taken by "a narrow circle of people," often without proper consultation with "friends" and without a "collective, comprehensive examination or analysis." There were "errors and miscalculations." As a result, foreign policy consisted of military actions rather than political responses. The consequences had been deleterious. The Soviet Union had been perceived as a military threat, and its progressive intentions were misunderstood. Moreover, objections to Soviet military actions were expressed even by socialist countries and socialist parties. (Both Romania and Yugoslavia had denounced the Brezhnev Doctrine, which was invoked to justify the invasion of Czechoslovakia in 1968. The Communist parties of Europe were also critical of the decision.) There was considerable loss of goodwill in the Third World as well, particularly as a result of the invasion of Afghanistan in 1979. Again, the military orientation implied that critical resources were diverted from the needs of the civilian economy, which must now take center stage.

In this characteristically bold and searching statement, Gorbachev was going one step further than in 1987 when he spoke at the seventieth anniversary celebration of the Bolshevik Revolution. There, he had been content to question the stereotypes of the Communist dogma, to pave the way for a view of the capitalist West that would permit him to take a more accommodating approach on military confrontation. Challenging the notions that capitalist nations cannot function without a bloated military sector, that they must necessarily exploit the Third World, and that they cannot coexist in peace with Communist countries, he had asked pointedly: If the West had served as a dependable partner in the fight against Nazism, why could it not be trusted to cooperate in safeguarding peace in the nuclear age? Superpower interdependence was then the theme. In June 1988, foreign policy was presented as a means to serve pressing domestic needs as well.

General Secretary Gorbachev has therefore challenged the very fundamentals of traditional foreign-policy formulation in the Soviet Union. But his task in bringing about change in this area is far from simple. As with the domestic reform program, there are supporters and detractors. Indeed, among the reformers, Dashichev had argued even before the June Conference for an accommodating role for foreign policy, contending that a favorable international atmosphere should be ensured for a profound restructuring of the Soviet economy and its political and social system. Bovin had suggested a radical change in the process of foreign policy formulation by proposing that it be opened up for public evaluation. Such scrutiny should not be limited to "certain episodes in the history of our foreign policy activity." By far the most original lessons from the record have been drawn by the ever-innovative Georgii Arbatov, director of the Institute for the Study of the United States and Canada and an influential adviser. He has proposed that foreign policy should be formulated by both superpowers to serve domestic interests. The U.S. policymakers, too, with an economy overburdened by huge military expenditures, budget deficits, and serious social and "ethnic" problems, must turn inward and start their own perestroika. These refreshing, pragmatic suggestions are being rebutted by conventional ideologues, among them Yegor Ligachev. Invoking the class character of international relations, he has proclaimed (*Pravda*, August 6, 1988) that Marxist, national liberation struggles abroad are legitimate and deserve support.

NEW INITIATIVES

The new thinking has already prompted new initiatives. These are mainly manifest in the Third World and in the renewed détente symbolized by the Intermediate Nuclear Forces (INF) Treaty that General Secretary Gorbachev and President Reagan signed at the 1988 Moscow Summit. There are nuanced changes in the Soviet role in Eastern Europe as well.

The Third World

Gorbachev's predecessors had seen their influence diminish in recent years in the Third World. The agenda of activity that was initiated with Khrushchev's announcement of "peaceful coexistence" with the West had lost its momentum toward the end of the Brezhnev leadership. This was not merely because of military failures. It was, rather, a product of the diminished appeal of the Soviet planned system as a role model; the reduced Soviet capacity to provide needed economic support had also played a role. What had changed to bring this about?

The Soviet Union was a role model for several developing countries in the 1940s and the 1950s. Its emphasis on planned acceleration of growth rates, its success at rapid industrialization, and the egalitarian ideology that seemed to characterize its economy had ready appeal to many leaders of newly independent countries. They too sought rapid economic growth with social justice. By now, the Soviet miracle is perceived as a mirage. The spectacle of the Soviet Union and China scrambling to escape the consequences of their economic organization only reinforces the skepticism with which developing countries view the advantages of these economic systems. The Soviet Union is no longer a role model, to put it mildly.

At the same time, it has ceased to be a major, alternative source of technology and credit for the Third World. In the 1950s, when U.S. policymakers could not override domestic economic and ideological lobbies to finance heavy industry and oil refining projects in the public sector in countries such as India, the Soviet Union won accolades by stepping into the vacuum. Since its development strategy emphasized these areas, the Soviet Union had precisely the technology and skills that were needed by these developing countries.

The scene has changed altogether now. The development strategies and needs are different. The emphasis has shifted to agriculture, exports, and high tech, and the Soviet Union is not considered to be competent at any of these activities. The Soviet Union, and indeed the Soviet bloc, is not even a credible source of funds and technology for the Third World; it has itself become a net borrower in the world's capital markets and an eager recipient of foreign technologies to boost its failing growth rate. In fact, the Soviet bloc's borrowings in the last decade and a half must have "crowded out" some Third World borrowing.

There is little that Gorbachev can do to change this, at least until perestroika has succeeded over the long haul. However, Gorbachev has been able to alter the Soviet role in the Third World by beginning to close out Soviet military and quasi-military involvements in Afghanistan, Angola, and Cambodia. Soviet troops are withdrawing from Afghanistan, more or less on schedule. Cuba and Vietnam, two allies, are being persuaded, if not pressured, to switch from military modes of operation—the former in Angola, the latter in Cambodia. The fifty thousand Cuban forces propping up the Marxist regime in Angola may gradually be withdrawn in return for a South African grant of independent status to neighboring Namibia. The decade-long occupation of Cambodia by Vietnamese forces is scheduled to end by 1990. With the withdrawal of Soviet soldiers from Afghanistan and of Vietnamese soldiers from Cambodia, Gorbachev is also improving the prospects of a reconciliation with China (which still demands, as its price, the removal of Soviet soldiers from the Chinese border).

One may interpret these moves as simply the product of fatigue induced by protracted conflicts with unyielding foes. But credit must be given also to those whose material support enabled these foes to resist Soviet firepower, and to Gorbachev, who decided boldly to end the anguish rather than procrastinate and persist. Of course, despite the military winding down, Soviet sales of military hardware to the Third World, which have run close to U.S. sales in recent years, will continue.

Eastern Europe

Gorbachev's task in Eastern Europe is not quite that simple. The region has posed problems of political control and management for the Soviets ever since Winston Churchill spoke in 1946 of the "iron curtain" dividing Europe. Almost three decades later, in August 1975, Leonid Brezhnev's Soviet Union and thirty-five states of Europe and North America would sign the Helsinki Agreement that formally recognized the postwar boundaries of Europe, but the political problems of managing Eastern Europe would not diminish.

Eastern Europe has traditionally been controlled with diverse techniques, appropriate to the conditions in each "satellite" nation. The critical and overriding concern has always been that, whatever these countries did, the one-party Communist system should not be threatened and that there should not be any move away from Soviet hegemony. While the result of Tito's defiance of Stalin in 1947 was the beginning of an alternative Communist voice in Europe, over the years, the worker-managed Yugoslav economy has continued to embrace a one-party system and has not invited Soviet retribution. Romania, while asserting its independence with Moscow, has remained nonetheless a faithful, if brutal, specimen of socialism.

By contrast, Soviet tanks marched into Budapest in 1956. Not only were the plans for reforming the economy revolutionary, but the proposals under Nagy's leadership for Hungary's withdrawal from the Warsaw Pact threatened the unity of the bloc and the future of communism. More dangerous were the nascent changes in Czechoslovakia under Dubček's leadership involving reform of the party and the government, and relaxed censorship. Those were exhilarating days in Prague in the spring of 1968. By August, however, Czechoslovakia was invaded by forces of the Warsaw Pact. Dubček's reforms, somewhat similar to the current Soviet reforms under Gorbachev, were out of time and out of place. Dubček was retired; so was one-third of the party membership—500,000 in all.

The deteriorating situation in Poland, where worker defiance has sometimes reached foolhardy levels, also invited Soviet intervention, but at arm's length, and has eluded definitive solutions. The waves of consumer protest and labor unrest, culminating in the establishment of Solidarity in August 1980 under Lech Walesa's leadership, gathered such momentum as to seriously threaten the stability of the Communist state. Paradoxically, a genuine broad-based proletarian movement with popular support was threatening to topple a Communist regime, whereas Marxism had predicted that the proletariat would overthrow a bourgeois-capitalist system. In December 1981, Solidarity was outlawed and Gierek was removed by General Jaruzelski, but Polish workers and the populace in general would continue to be at odds with the regime. Gorbachev would inherit a Poland not at peace with itself.

Gorbachev's objectives for Eastern Europe have not changed dramatically. Everything points to his wanting to retain the Leninist model of a one-party state. Nor can he want these countries to fall away from Soviet hegemonic influence. Yet there are changes of interest and importance. In the wake of perestroika and glasnost' at home, Gorbachev has acknowledged the need for cultural variety and political diversity in Eastern Europe. Unity does not mean uniformity, nor is there a single "model" of socialism to be emulated by everyone. This acknowledgment at the June Party Conference, plus the new skepticism about military solutions that I discussed earlier, increases the possibility of a fresh breeze in Eastern Europe without Soviet repression.

The pace of political reform in Eastern Europe, however, will continue to be slower than in the Soviet Union. This is partly because of prudence. Given the two constraints emanating from Gorbachev—the continuation of the one-party state and Soviet hegemony—prudence requires that the necessary fine-tuning be achieved by keeping at least a step or two behind Gorbachev's own reforms. The East Europeans must live with the circumstances of geography and history that make the Soviets a forbidding presence. If they could behave freely, they would emulate the Bulgarian in the story circulating in Sophia involving a Finn, a Russian, and a Bulgarian on top of a tower. The three are told to follow a local custom and discard something that they have gotten used to. The Finn pulls out a bottle of vodka from his jacket and empties it ever so reluctantly. The Russian takes the party membership card from his wallet and tears it up. The Bulgarian promptly catches hold of the Russian and throws him off the tower.

But it is not prudence alone that will keep the pace of change in much of Eastern Europe behind that in the Soviet Union. Few of the local Communist Party bosses in Bulgaria, Romania, and East Germany, for instance, are bursting with enthusiasm to introduce political changes that would limit the arbitrary power they have enjoyed under the current regime. They will move only if Gorbachev's example encourages their populations to push for such reforms for themselves, and to the extent that Gorbachev himself seeks to stimulate and disseminate these changes in the bloc that he leads.

Arms Control

The dramatic achievement in foreign policy initiatives is the INF Treaty of 1988, which targets all intermediate-range missiles for destruction. Gorbachev certainly played a major role in achieving this breakthrough, despite the complexities of the arms control negotiations and an ever-watchful adversary in President Reagan. True, he had the edge over the President in that he faced fewer constraints from his Warsaw Pact allies. But Gorbachev was the spitting image of a superb tactician on a winning streak. He acted the "maximalist" negotiator who starts with an untenable initial package and makes concessions at intervals in such a way that each concession appears as a spectacular initiative. His position at the Reykjavik summit in October 1986 was that the proposed 50-percent reduction in strategic nuclear weapons could not be separated from consideration of Reagan's SDI initiative, nor from a possible deal on intermediate-range missiles. His offer in early March 1987 to negotiate a separate INF treaty, eventually signed and sealed at the Moscow summit, came as a startling surprise and was perceived as a statesmanlike initiative.

Interestingly, the tactic of continuing surprises that unfreeze long-held positions has been used in other initiatives as well. In mid-June 1988, Gorbachev's representatives tabled a package of proposals on conventional arms. Exchange and verification of information on the forces of NATO and the Warsaw Pact would precede the withdrawal of 500,000 men from the territory of each alliance and the retirement of "offensive" weapons such as tanks and artillery. Then, in mid-September, Gorbachev offered a soufflé with much air and less substance: the Krasnoyarsk radar installation, which, in the official U.S. view, violates the 1972 Anti-ballistic Missile (ABM) Treaty, could be converted for use in peaceful exploration of space under international supervision, and Soviet naval forces at Cam Ranh Bay in Vietnam could be removed, in exchange for the removal of U.S. military bases in the Philippines.

Needless to say, this flurry of unceasing initiatives in the arms control arena have won for Gorbachev the admiration of many around the world. Public opinion polls in Europe reveal that Gorbachev's image as a peacemaker is way ahead of Reagan's. Prime Minister Margaret Thatcher, who sees in Gorbachev a man in her image, boldly restructuring an economy on the skids much as she has done, once said approvingly: "We can do business with him." Now she says grudgingly: "How does one handle the Russian bear when it smiles?"

The question arises: What precisely has motivated Gorbachev's efforts at arms control? The answer has to be multifaceted. The shift from preoccupation with militarism as the sensible response to security needs is certainly a contributory factor here. Gorbachev put it directly at the June Party Conference: "In seeking strategic military parity, we did not always in the past exploit opportunities for safeguarding state security by political means. As a result we allowed ourselves to be drawn into an arms race that was bound to affect the country's socioeconomic development and its international status" (*Pravda*, June 29, 1988). In his view, arms control represents a viable and more efficient method of maintaining security: "A part of our foreign policy credo is a willingness to terminate mutually the presence of foreign forces and bases on foreign territories" (*Pravda*, June 29, 1988). The economic gains to be made by controlling the expensive arms race have certainly been a major input in this equation. Nor is Gorbachev's willingness to negotiate unrelated to Reagan's arms buildup and the Strategic Defense Initiative (SDI). Surely, the cost of an arms race was increased by the alarming prospect of having to counter SDI with an appropriate response.

How substantial and speedy are the savings in resources from arms control agreements likely to be? It is important to note that the savings of military expenditures resulting from the agreements to date are small, whereas those from future agreements will be slow in coming. The INF Treaty, for example, extends only to 5 percent of the existing nuclear forces on both sides. The prospect of containing new expenditures on space-based research in response to SDI is still beyond Gorbachev's horizon, as the new U.S. administration is likely to continue R & D expenditures on it, albeit at reduced levels approved by the Congress. Large savings can accrue from a reduction of conventional forces in Europe. Here the Warsaw Pact dominates NATO by a ratio of about 3 to 1 in tanks, 2 to 1 in combat aircraft, 2 to 1 in artillery pieces, and 4 or 5 to 1 in short-range nuclear missiles. The savings are predicated on Soviet willingness to accept a more than proportional cut in the various categories. As for the 50-percent reduction in strategic forces currently under negotiation, the prospects for an equitable and verifiable reduction are clouded by Soviet domination in mobile missiles. There is also a related problem: the signing of the INF Treaty abolishing intermediate-range missiles from Europe leaves the nuclear defense of Europe to nuclear weapons based in the United States or at sea, since NATO has very few short-range missiles. Therefore, from the U.S.-European perspective, it would be unsafe to reach an agreement on a 50-percent reduction of strategic weapons unless and until the Soviet superiority of conventional forces in Europe (including short-range missiles) is corrected by their relatively larger reduction. Will the Soviet negotiators make that concession? Indeed, the road to future arms control agreements is paved with major hurdles.

How large are the direct Soviet savings from reduced commitments in the Third World? These include economic and military aid and the costs of military actions such as those in Afghanistan and Angola. Economic aid commitments to Cuba and Vietnam in 1985 amounted to about $5.7 billion. Similar aid in 1985 for the non-Communist Third World came close to $3 billion (Central Intelligence Agency 1987, 113, 115–16). The annual military cost of supporting the Marxist government in Angola amounted to $1 billion (*Wall Street Journal*, July 29, 1988). The Soviet military activity in Afghanistan is reported to have cost $1.7 million a day (*Economist*, April 1, 1988, 58). These are by no means negligible amounts. They have prompted Gorbachev to take a hard look at the drain in resources that their continuation would involve.

The next question to consider is, How large will the gains be to the Soviet economy as resources are pulled from foreign commitments to domestic uses and, especially, from military use to the civilian sector? In particular, recall Arbatov's suggestion that both superpowers should divert men and materials from military use to civilian production. Here the contrasts are illuminating. In the United States, where economic organization is more flexible and market-responsive, the returns from the switch can be expected to be higher—unless, of course, the scale of change is so enormous that "adjustment" problems arise, leading to a high degree of transitional unemployment and related difficulties. Again, while the U.S. military-industrial complex has its deleterious implications, it is marked by the private ownership of productive capacities, ensuring the incentive to convert capacities to new civilian uses as military demands diminish. The Soviet arrangements differ on both these counts. Where resources are completely switched, the returns will be less because Soviet productivity will continue to be low, given the limited economic scope of perestroika. Second, the state-owned military-industrial sector may choose to maintain flexible dual-purpose capacities rather than convert completely to civilian use. Perhaps Gorbachev's commitment to arms control will finally eradicate the "readiness is all" syndrome from the military establishment.

But major economic gains can accrue indirectly. The atmosphere of détente has certainly been revived, thanks to Gorbachev's initiatives, in foreign policy abroad and through glasnost' at home. Europe, in particular, has begun to respond to the opportunity for economic and technological participation. And, as I discuss in the next chapter, détente offers Gorbachev's Soviet Union the prospect for renewed credits and an influx of technological know-how. All this can yield *quick* economic benefits that the modest reforms in the domestic economy cannot provide to a populace eager for tangible rewards from perestroika.*

---

* Let me explain. Suppose Gorbachev's planners are able to borrow $1 billion from the West because of renewed détente. This money can be used for importing sophisticated machines, or consumer goods that are in short supply. There are thus fairly immediate benefits to the economy. The alternative for the planners is to earn $1 billion by first producing something at home and then exporting it to the United States or another hard-currency country. With this approach, the planners face the problem of soft oil prices in export markets and current Soviet inability to export manufactured goods to Western markets. From this perspective, the strategy of borrowing rather than exporting has a distinct edge. And it is, indeed, succeeding. According to a report (*New York Times*, October 21, 1988), European banks have signaled their intention to lend more than $9 billion to the Soviet Union in the coming months.

The Strategy of Reform

GORBACHEV'S REFORMS therefore appear to be substantial and rapid on the noneconomic and foreign-policy fronts, limited and even inadequately conceived on the economic front, and guarded on the political front. By contrast, the Chinese reforms under Deng Xiaoping, while unyielding in politics, have been haphazard on the noneconomic front but substantive in the economic area. Is there a strategic design here?[4] It is important to answer this question. It bears on whether perestroika can succeed and on the way it can be expected to develop.

Since reforms of the perestroika variety are "systemic" in intent, and since Gorbachev is attempting more than cosmetic changes, he must confront interest groups that are committed to the pre-perestroika regime. In so doing, he must therefore have a sense of strategy as to the pace, composition, and sequencing of his reforms. The wrong sequencing, for instance, could imperil the program. Gorbachev could be inviting serious problems if he were to attempt first the reforms that take on sizable vested interests, instead of focusing on changes that avoid such confrontations. Such considerations surely account for Gorbachev's initial emphasis on substantive noneconomic reforms accompanied by only limited economic reforms.

NONECONOMIC VERSUS ECONOMIC REFORMS

Noneconomic reforms, including freer expression of opinion, expansion of religious freedom, and continuing relaxation of emigration restrictions, among others, have twofold *immediate* advantages in Gorbachev's new war on the old regime, neither of them shared by Deng Xiaoping.

First, the United States in particular (and the West to a lesser degree) sees progress in human rights, and hence reform of the kind Gorbachev is introducing, as an important piece of evidence that the Soviet Union is changing from its propensity for acting like an "evil empire." It strengthens the hands of those abroad who would restore détente, facilitates arms control, contributes to a lowering of defense expenditures, and leads to renewed inflows of foreign credits, investments, and technology—all to Soviet advantage.

Deng Xiaoping has no such benefits to gain from similar reforms. The fact is that Chinese violations of human rights, as egregious as in the Soviet Union, simply do not attract the opprobrium associated with Soviet handling of human rights. Several factors combine to produce this asymmetrical outcome.

The Soviet émigrés, a vocal community, are critical of the Soviet regime; so are the émigrés of the East European nations. Not so the overseas Chinese community, which acts more as if it was part of a diaspora seeking identification with the Chinese regime. The emigration issue is explosive for the Soviet Union primarily because of the unrelenting concern of world Jewry. The Chinese leadership has no such element to deal with. The emigration issue is also double-edged in relation to China; as the Chinese know very well, U.S. policymakers have little interest in forcing an issue that could lead to a significant increase in the substantial tide of refugees and migrants trying to get to America. Deng Xiaoping is alleged to have remarked wryly: "How many million Chinese would you like us to allow to emigrate to the United States?" Again, there is probably an element of self-indulgent unconcern about Chinese failings on human rights. The Chinese, after all, are the foes of our principal adversary and rival. Finally, there is perhaps the residual legacy of the benign view of a benevolent "oriental despotism," from which China has benefited since the eighteenth century. All in all, Chinese denials of human rights are not seen in the same stark colors as the Soviet failings.

Second, Gorbachev clearly is letting freedoms develop apace because they create domestic allies as well. The population at large has developed a stake in perestroika because it has already tasted the fruits of Gorbachev's determination. Economic reforms simply could not have generated these allies; in fact, they can often create opposition. The supporters of the popular noneconomic component of the reforms can be of vital importance to the success of Gorbachev's total program.

THE NATURE AND SEQUENCING OF ECONOMIC REFORMS

But what about the strategic thinking underlying the economic reforms themselves? The design of an efficient strategy is essential here also. The sequencing must carefully negotiate the minefield of opposing vested interests. It is critical to focus initially on reforms that are likely to cause minimal disruption to any substantial group in the short run. The garnering of early victories would ensure both credibility and a good foundation for further, more difficult, reform. The gradualism implied in this approach must be combined with clear articulation of ultimate objectives by the leadership, so that the inevitable tactical retreats in the course of unfolding reforms are not interpreted as abandonment of the economic war itself, compromising the entire experiment.

Gorbachev appears to have an intuitive understanding of these strategic principles, as I will now explain. There remain, however, certain oddities and puzzles. These in turn suggest possible improvements in the strategy as revealed by the decisions and pronouncements to date.

Liberalization in Developing Countries

Let me begin by noting that the Soviet reforms have certain parallels with the "liberalization" packages that have characterized attempts at economic reform in several developing countries. The latter are typically imposed by external agencies such as the International Monetary Fund and the

World Bank. By contrast, the Soviet reforms, like the recent Chinese and the Indian efforts, are endogenously designed and promoted.

The liberalization packages typically contain several microeconomic elements. Where stabilization is involved, as in many South American countries, macroeconomic reforms are also included. The former, which have relevance to the Soviet case, generally involve the features that follow.

PUBLIC SECTOR ENTERPRISES

Nearly all developing countries have large public sectors in the form of industrial enterprises and utilities. These are publicly owned. Often they run at losses, which are covered by state subsidies. Where inflation is a problem, they contribute to macroeconomic difficulties, reducing overall savings and compromising the growth effort. The automatic subsidization also implies that there are inefficiencies in production due to lack of market discipline. Additionally, many public sector enterprises, almost everywhere, are subject to political interference resulting in overstaffing and other such sources of inefficiency in operation. Two options are available to developing-country reformers for dealing with the situation. They can aim at second-best improvements in the functioning of public sector enterprises. These often amount to exhortations or commitments that fly in the face of political realities. Official pronouncements that these enterprises should be freed from political interference are an excellent, if exasperating, example of such unrealistic, purely symbolic reform. The best solution is privatization.

THE PRIVATE SECTOR

The private sector, on the other hand, usually suffers from policies that encourage the wrong activities. For example, the overvalued exchange rates lead to wasteful import substitution. Price controls on food for urban consumers adversely affect food producers and output. There is also a maze of stifling controls on economic activity. For example, existing capacities cannot be expanded nor can new capacities be set up without prior approval. Imports too are allocated via government licenses. No wonder then that resources, including entrepreneurial energies, are diverted to unproductive activity in search of profits by evading or avoiding controls and by influencing them.

The opposition to implementing reforms in the developing countries arises from different directions. In regard to public sector reforms, conventional left-wing intellectuals driven by ideology can provide the opposition. So can politicians and bureaucrats who see that their patronage will be curtailed if controls and allocations are replaced by market signals or outright privatization. The loss of subsidies can also mean higher prices to final consumers. This can ignite protests and riots, as Ghana, Egypt, and Poland have discovered.[5]

As for private sector reforms, these imply adjustment costs as resources are pulled from inefficient to efficient producers. Everyone must then respond to incentives that are more in line with appropriate prices. The adjustment costs arise because real wage rigidities often lead to unemployment in industries in which profitability is reduced. The opposition therefore typically arises from labor unions and also from producers who face losses and must fold their operations.

But this is not the end of the story. In many developing countries, the private sector has functioned under a set of rules that automatically protect existing producers against the winds of change. Their profitability is cushioned through strict import controls and, in some cases, through regulated entry, even by domestic rivals, into a protected activity. The private sector therefore is run by rentiers (who enjoy "squatters' rights") rather than by Schumpeterian entrepreneurs (who take risks). Economic reform of the liberalization variety often involves taking on this aspect of the private sector as well. In that case the opposition will come from the "iron quartet," consisting of

(1) politicians who would lose the patronage and profits that result from operating, and often selling, investment and import licenses to these rentiers; (2) the producers themselves, who are used to working within a system that, after granting the necessary license, guarantees profits and a quiet life; (3) labor unions that are happy to get a share of the rents rather than take the risks of losing jobs in a market-oriented system where firms can exit much more freely;[6] and (4) policymakers who are attached to the old ways and feel threatened by the challenge to their conventional wisdom.

The Soviet Case

Soviet economic reforms face similar challenges. But the differences are important, too. Two dominant features of the Soviet system bear on the parallels and contrasts.

First, the Soviet public sector is all-encompassing, its raison d'être being the Marxist tenet of public ownership of the means of production. By contrast, the public sector in the non-Communist developing world is limited, by and large, to heavy industry and public utilities. Other industries, agriculture, services, and trade are not publicly owned. This contrast means that Gorbachev does not have to contend with the private sector's vested interests the way the prime minister of a non-Communist developing country must.[7] On the other hand, Gorbachev faces different, but nevertheless serious, constraints in dealing with the public sector. In developing countries, the growth of the public sector has been legitimated by arguments that have been a ragbag of the desire to promote equality, regional balance, a preferred pattern of economic growth via the ownership of heavy industry, and so on. The inspiration may have come from Fabian socialism or Soviet Marxism but, in general, there are chinks in the ideological armor. Capitalist markets and even privatization may therefore be introduced in small, decisive doses without challenging ideology and creating a political crisis. Gorbachev cannot afford that luxury; public ownership is a serious matter in the Soviet Union, a central tenet of the regime.

Second, there is the dominance of the single Communist Party. Along with the subservience of countervailing actors such as the media, this may suggest that Gorbachev should have less difficulty with his reform battles than his counterparts in developing countries. Perhaps so; but the pulls and pressures turn into intraparty struggles, and Gorbachev's advantages are then less obvious. The key fact remains that, in carrying the party with him, Gorbachev will have to be mindful of its interests—and these interests have been secured by party control of the traditional working of the centrally planned economy in all its aspects.

The consequences of these differences, defined by public ownership of the means of production and the dominance of the Communist Party, are manifest in Gorbachev's reform strategy. His first strategic decision has been to cover his ideological flanks and defuse intellectual opposition from those who wear Suslov's mantle by defining the limits of perestroika accordingly. In my judgment, Gorbachev himself is strongly committed to the socialist tradition; his pronouncements to date suggest that. But the fact that this position strengthens his hand while weakening the content of perestroika is doubtless of strategic significance.

Even within this constraint, Gorbachev has taken the further precaution of excluding reforms that would risk alienating important groups. Thus, prices are to be managed and set from above, at least until the price reform promised in 1990.[8] The substantial gains to be made by price flexibility in response to changing supplies and demands will therefore not be tapped.[9] Gorbachev and his advisers evidently fear the possibility of price rises in key consumer items and have decided to forgo this reform. Economic reform is marked, in its beginning phase at least, by the far more limited nonprice flexibility implied by the "demand-determined" contract regime that I discussed earlier. Little is ventured, and little gained in consequence.

The official sanctioning of cooperatives in consumer goods and services and several manufacturing activities is also a relatively riskless and potentially popular reform. It introduces flexibility, and a form of capital and labor mobility, that is not meaningfully achievable within the constraints imposed by state ownership. This reform, as I noted earlier, can be seen as an attempt at legalizing the enormous "second" economy that has grown as an offshoot of the planned economy. In so doing, it does expand this sector and its potential benefits by eliminating its shadowy status and hence the resource waste that is usually part of undertaking illegal and quasi-legal activities in the presence of enforcement by the state.

In increasing the availability of consumer goods and also legitimating private economic activity (albeit within the cooperative organizational structure), this reform cannot but be popular, as it is gradually proving to be. But again this tail cannot wag the dog. Its impact can only be limited unless and until a sizable share of investment and production is organized in this sector rather than in the state-owned sector. But as long as the latter remains a key tenet of Soviet socialism, it is difficult to imagine how the cooperative sector can be allowed to grow enough to offer meaningful rewards to significant numbers of participants. The politics of socialism, in the end, defines the limits on the gains that the economics of perestroika can yield.

Gorbachev's economic reforms are therefore, deliberately and strategically in all likelihood, modest and cautious. His initial steps aim at early but limited rewards and seek to minimize adverse reactions from key pressure groups that would mobilize if perestroika's economic content was more ambitious.

If one were to fault the Gorbachev strategy at all, it would be in two areas: the slow pace of reform in agriculture and the tolerance of occasional acute shortages of critical consumer goods. Though, even here, the latest developments have begun to repair these omissions. Let me explain.

An important empirical observation about economic reforms in Communist nations—Hungary and China are prime examples—is that agricultural reforms usually precede reforms in other sectors, especially in industry. The inefficiencies of communes and collective and state farms in Communist agriculture are overwhelming. Reform consists primarily of creating private plots or independent cooperatives with incentives to grow and sell one's own output. Hardly any group is hurt by this: farmers are happier, food output increases and prices fall for buyers in other sectors, the "wage-goods" bottleneck to industrial investment (if any) is eased, and so on. If the party functionaries can be diverted to other pursuits, as in China and Hungary, agricultural reform is a splendid example of a positive-sum-game reform in Communist countries. (This is evidently not true of significant industrial reforms, which can hurt important groups. Nor is it true of agricultural reform in developing countries, where reform involves eliminating absentee landlords, granting security of tenure to tenancy farmers, breaking up unwieldy farms, and so forth—measures that often pit one group [e.g., landlords] against another.)

Gorbachev somehow hesitated, as I discussed earlier (chapter 5), on the agricultural front. Perhaps he knew from his personal experience in agriculture prior to his rise to national leadership that, unlike the situation in China and Hungary, the party was significantly entrenched in the countryside and constituted a bottleneck to rapid and substantial progress. Perhaps an obsession with mechanization and fertilizer absorption as a "technological" solution to Soviet agriculture's problems may also have been the reason for not introducing incentives and economic reform. In any event, Gorbachev appeared certainly to have broken, most likely to his disadvantage, from the agriculture-most and agriculture-first pattern of economic reform in Communist lands. However, his latest initiatives aimed at promoting leases of up to fifty years for individual farm families represent a major step forward in agricultural reform and constitute a recognition of the importance of agriculture in his overall reform strategy.

As for the shortages of consumer goods, whether they have increased and whether perestroika has contributed to the problem are debatable. But following glasnost' and demokratizatsiia, shortages have been seen and heard of more frequently. One must not lose sight of the fact that the phenomenon of a Soviet leader, besieged by his people with complaints at a street corner, is altogether new. Ironically, the Soviet motto seems to have changed from "Not by bread alone" to "Not by freedom alone." So far the use of foreign exchange and gold sales as a tactical device for shoring up perestroika by strategically importing manufactured consumer goods so as to relieve scarcities of key items has been avoided. But even this lapse in astute policy management is being corrected. Thus, a major part of the $1.6 billion credit announced by German banks in October 1988 is to be used for renovating Soviet food processing and consumer goods industries.

I think therefore it is fair to conclude that the sequencing of the economic reforms is sensible: Gorbachev has a fine strategic sense. Of course, none of this careful consideration and caution in devising and implementing perestroika's economic component assures the ultimate success of the planned change. There are bound to be problems as the system changes gears, however slowly. For instance, the *Economist* (May 28, 1988, 63) notes:

> There has not been any rush to open new co-operative restaurants or cafeterias, or to take over old loss-making ones on an agency basis, despite enormous unsatisfied demand. Some of the thwarted restaurateurs blame this on the bureaucracy's obsessions with plans that are dottily imposed even upon new entrepreneurial ventures, and insistence on a myriad of regulations and audits.
>
> A franker reason is that state catering workers—who might otherwise become restaurateurs—at present make a good living by pilfering and reselling on the black market all of the

Fig. 8.1. Mikhail Gorbachev, in the midst of an articulate crowd in Krasnoyarsk in September 1988. He has broken the mold of Soviet politics by reaching out to the people. AFP photo.

nicest foods in short supply. If they were in the private sector their incomes would fall because it is not profitable to steal from your own business.

But it is also necessary not to exaggerate the consequences of these difficulties. If Gorbachev remains in control, there could be increasing pressure to eliminate the "myriad of regulations and audits," just as the early intentions of taxing the cooperative sector's profits at exorbitant rates have yielded to better sense. Moreover, is it meaningful to think in terms of a limited supply of restaurateurs? After all, as we all know, restaurants open and close at a phenomenal rate wherever there is free entry and exit. In fact, this tendency to equate initial difficulties with the final outcome and hence to assign perestroika, even in its limited present format, to premature demise, is manifest in other areas of planned reform. Thus, Robert Kaiser (*Washington Post, National Weekly*, June 6–12, 1988, 24) writes skeptically of agricultural reforms, not because they are limited but because they face the bottleneck of unresponsive farmers:

> Breaking the old taboos of Soviet life, particularly the institutionalized lying and hiding of facts, is probably much easier than—for example—teaching peasants to grow more food. Many here talk of agricultural reform as potentially the most rewarding change that can be made quickly. The idea is to create Soviet farmers, relying on family units that assume responsibility for a plot of land and profit from their labors in direct proportion to the crops they produce. This notion is vaguely enshrined in official pronouncements, and new laws make it at least plausible, but it is not yet widely practiced in the countryside.
>
> The critical factor for success, of course, is the peasants' willingness to take responsibility. But these peasants never had any responsibility; neither did their forbears. The successful Russian farmers of the early years of this century were literally wiped out in Stalin's collectivization campaign; what remained were the poorest farm hands who have now spent generations as hired laborers on state and collective farms. They have no tradition of family farming, and American specialists in Soviet agriculture say there is excellent reason to doubt that reforms will produce the desired result any time soon.

This fear is reminiscent of the fallacy that development economists had to lay to rest three decades ago—that developing country farmers would or could not respond to price incentives. We now know better; so should the fortunately anonymous "American specialists" whom Kaiser relies on for his skepticism.

The caution in circumscribing the scope of change and its slowness in taking hold suggest that Gorbachev would be well advised not to promise significant immediate economic results from his perestroika. But I doubt if he needs this advice. For here too, he has shown an unusual awareness: he has repeatedly emphasized that instant economic gratification cannot follow from the reforms.[10] Like every politician, however, he must know that exhortations and education are not enough. Immediate improvements in living standards cannot be denied. They must somehow be financed. And here the noneconomic component of perestroika returns to center stage.

For, it is not with the reforms as such but rather with the reduced burden of defense expenditures following the arms control agreements, the reduction of external commitments through renewed détente, and the increase in the inflow of external technology and resources that would follow from these that Gorbachev expects to keep the populace happy. The two components of perestroika, the economic and the noneconomic, are therefore an integral whole.

I must finally raise a different but related question: Do the limited economic reforms have any prospect of eventually moving into higher gear? Gradualism is in order because, as I have argued, that is the only politically feasible route. A planned system cannot change gears suddenly. But the critical questions are, Do the planners intend taking the arrangements, eventually, even if step by step, to a market system? and, if that is so, What are the chances of their achieving that goal?

I have serious misgivings. There are two reasons.

First, there are genuine problems with the Soviet economists' comprehension of the market system, as I argued earlier (chapter 5). I am doubtful if their misconceptions can change enough to override their conventional thinking on these questions. Tinkering, even if substantial, is what the country will continue to get. Thus a new "Soviet Socialism" is likely to emerge, consisting of a socialist cake with capitalist icing.

Second, even if the Soviet planners were to want to introduce genuine, systemic economic reforms, this aspiration would eventually run into the problem of the twin requirements of the Communist state: overwhelming state ownership of the means of production and a one-party state. It is difficult to see how these can be reconciled with a functioning regime of profit motivation and criteria, free capital and labor markets, an open trading arrangement with meaningful exchange rates, and trading by "rule of law" rather than quantities.

A substantive question then remains: Is General Secretary Gorbachev, even with the program he has so far settled for, likely to survive? Where astrology fails, social scientists such as myself are helpless too: the future is unknowable. But the task is not altogether hopeless. We can bring our comprehension of the past and perception of the present to speculate on the course of the future. This is the aim of the final chapter.

How Long Will Gorbachev Last?

EVERYONE ACKNOWLEDGES that Mikhail Gorbachev has the leadership qualities for meeting the challenge of perestroika. His energy and charisma, his political savvy, above all his self-assurance as a leader in charge, are no longer in doubt. They were clearly visible at the June Party Conference. And yet the question persists: Will he last? It recurs every time the pot threatens to boil over, as during the El'tsin affair, the continuing Armenian-Azerbaijani clashes and, in particular, when the Ligachev-sponsored letter critical of the reform appeared in *Sovetskaia rossiia*.

A Soviet leader is made or unmade by the top brass of the party. The procedure is arbitrary in contrast with the election by popular vote of the leader of a party who then forms a government of like-minded colleagues. In a parliamentary democracy, the cabinet as a whole can be thrown out of power by a vote of no-confidence in the parliament, which consists of elected representatives. Short of that possibility, the prime minister rules the roost. Prime Minister Margaret Thatcher cannot be summarily removed from power by the machinations of only a few power brokers in her own party. On the other hand, there is always the possibility that the Politburo of the Communist Party can decide to remove General Secretary Gorbachev. At the same time, it is difficult to predict the configuration of circumstances that could result in such an outcome. The deliberations of the Politburo are conducted in total secrecy. Outside observers have no knowledge of the arguments put forth by members for and against a certain issue, although guesses abound.

No one seems more aware of the possibility of his ouster than Gorbachev. That is perhaps why, for all his dynamism and the appearance of a freewheeling style, Gorbachev is a stickler for procedures. He is evidently aware that perestroika cannot be launched and accomplished in an arbitrary, ad hoc fashion. A proreform consensus must be hammered out and maintained among the top brass of the party under his leadership. At every opportunity, likeminded comrades must be promoted to the Politburo and to secretaryships in the party's administrative apparatus. True, Gorbachev failed to get perestroika supporters elected to the Central Committee at the June Party Conference. But the reform of election 'procedures at all levels (aimed at introducing new blood into the party and the government) and the proposed change to a presidential form of government (with the potential for concentrating decision making in his hands) were approved by the Conference. The President is to be elected by an enlarged Congress of People's Deputies rather than by a handful of men in the Politburo. The suggestion by the actor Mikhail Ulyanov that the tenure of the President be fifteen years rather than the ten-year period proposed for everyone else was greeted by thunderous applause at the Conference. In short, Gorbachev has been busy creating a pro-Gorbachev, pro-perestroika consensus with admirable finesse and enormous patience. In this respect, he resembles a bourgeois politician in pursuit of consensus and a majority. Indeed, Gorbachev believes in this feature of demokratizatsiia. Thus, Trotsky had many faults, but the one the General Secretary singled out in his speech commemorating the seventieth anniversary of the Revolution was Trotsky's authoritarian, deceitful temperament. As for Stalin, Gorbachev asked how he could have adhered to democratic norms (a wolf might as well play the violin). Khrushchev, in his time, had brought in "winds of change," but Gorbachev described him as a "poor administrator," thus faulting him by implication for his inability to forge a consensus on his program and to implement it decisively. There is therefore an underlying strategy for maintaining cohesiveness under Gorbachev's leadership around a proreform consensus.

At no other time was this more apparent than in early October when Gorbachev carried out personnel changes in the party's top leadership. How to handle Yegor Ligachev, who has not been in full agreement with the pace of perestroika, with the sweeping changes in culture and history, or with the new thinking in foreign policy, has been a continuing problem. Ligachev represents the old guard and can certainly be expected to have followers throughout the party hierarchy and among the people. The strategy of maintaining consensus would suggest that Ligachev should be eased out gradually. It would be counterproductive, even risky, to expel him from the Politburo. Keeping him in the Politburo and putting him in charge of agriculture, on the other hand, would test his survivability to the utmost. That was what Gorbachev did. Then there was Viktor Chebrikov, another adversary and head of the KGB, who not only sat on a mountain of dossiers with valuable information about one and all but also controlled the institutional base for using it. He too was retained in the Politburo but removed as head of the KGB and put in charge of legal reform—undoubtedly a critical portfolio but also a challenging one. Perhaps Chebrikov's conservative impulses will be useful in keeping a lid on the law-and-order situation, which must occasionally worry Gorbachev himself. As for the retirement of Gromyko and Gorbachev's elevation, by a vote of the Supreme Soviet, to the presidency, which is still a ceremonial post, the clear signal was that Gorbachev will eventually be elected President, with enormous powers in domestic and foreign matters, when the political reforms finally become part of the Constitution. These personnel changes are obviously in line with Gorbachev's strategy of maintaining a proreform consensus under his leadership.

There is further evidence that Gorbachev is seeking a proreform consensus. First, in the Leninist tradition, Gorbachev gives a scientific basis to the changes he is proposing. He is not only a good communicator; he is also a first-rate theoretician. The proposed changes are logically presented as acceptable departures within the continuing tradition of Marxism-Leninism. Much has been said about Khrushchev's "voluntarism" and "subjectivism." Burlatsky (1988, 14) put it succinctly: " 'Khrushchevism,' as a concept of the renewal of socialism, was absent." By contrast, Gorbachev seeks to make his reforms highly acceptable by articulating their theoretical underpinnings.

Second, while the media is not totally at Gorbachev's beck and call, it is largely so. Gorbachev believes in keeping a finger on the public pulse. He has also made it possible for the people to voice their opinions and complaints. The dialogue on perestroika between the leader and the citizens, while carefully navigated, is so liberating that it must contribute positively to perestroika's success.

But the overriding factor favoring Gorbachev's success is that the reforms he is proposing are feasible. While I regard his reforms in the "superstructure" as bolder than those in the economy, they constitute a package that can be persuasively argued as necessary and feasible. He is not suggesting that the Soviet Union dump socialism and the plan, and embrace capitalism and the market. As I have argued, the reforms in politics and foreign policy, in the arts and literature, in the media, law, and education, are aimed at eradicating the vestiges of arrangements that are mostly outdated and sometimes tyrannical. As for the place of the market in the economic reforms, it can at best be described as tiptoeing on the threshold. All in all, I would characterize Gorbachev as an "extreme centrist"; his reforms therefore have a fair chance of acceptance.

But if the reforms are structured in a manner calculated to induce consent, the pace of reform may nonetheless provoke dissent. Gorbachev's fate may well be imperiled by the haste urged by impatient supporters, which may have been the case when the El'tsin affair exploded in Moscow. It is still not known what El'tsin said. Indeed glasnost' retains quite a bit of *skritnost'* (secretiveness). But many reports indicated that El'tsin wanted perestroika to move faster. Gorbachev's public reaction was revealing: he stressed the need for consensus, for a middle ground between the deviation of the "left" and the "right."

But then is there a possibility that, like Khrushchev, the now popular Gorbachev also may fall victim to the charge of developing the "cult of personality"? Demokratizatsiia and glasnost' are intended to foster a critical and open environment designed to keep everyone on his toes, including the General Secretary. But accountability is not the same as an absence of the cult. Nor can consensus building and collective leadership at the top preempt completely the emergence of a cult. Sholokhov is reported to have said about Stalin: "There was the cult, to be sure, but there was also the personality" (Burlatsky 1988, 14). This can be rephrased in relation to Gorbachev as: "There is the personality and there can, of course, be a cult." How can so energetic, charismatic, and visible a leader not be adulated? Khrushchev, for example, decried the cult of personality but was surrounded by sycophants. According to Burlatsky (1988, 14): "This man, a natural politician with a keen mind, at once bold and vigorous, was not free from the temptation to glorify himself. 'Our Nikita Sergeevich!' Wasn't that the beginning of the fall of the acknowledged fighter against the cult? Bootlickers drowned him in a deluge of flattery and adulation, receiving for their efforts high positions and awards, prizes and titles." The constraints have to be self-imposed. Gorbachev will have to walk a fine line and may be expected to have learned how from recent history.

It would therefore be surprising if Gorbachev falters and is retired. And tragic too—but more so for the Soviet Union than for Gorbachev. For while history belongs to the victors, there are rewards also for those who are vanquished in glorious wars. Nowhere is this better illustrated than by Medvedev's touching recall of Khrushchev's final brush in 1967 with the Central Committee for having allowed a French television crew to film his life in retirement: "At the interview, Kirillenko [who owed his promotion to the Presidium of the Central Committee to the ex-premier] snapped: 'You are still living too well.' Khrushchev's reply was measured. 'All right,' he said, 'you can take away my dacha and my pension. I shall be able

to wander through this country with my hand out-
stretched, and people will give me whatever I need. If
you were destitute, no one would give you anything' "
(Medvedev 1983, 254). Gorbachev can confidently expect
no less than Khrushchev from his countrymen.

Indeed, in the end, as they contemplate Gorbachev's
efforts, they may want to recall Tvardovsky's apt lines: "I
don't think we shall be taken to task in the next world for
not having done what we couldn't have done; but if we
could have done something and didn't—for that we will be
punished" (Lakshin 1980, 134). Should he succeed, their
thoughts could then turn to Robert Frost's verse:

> Two roads diverged in a wood,
> and I—
> I took the one less traveled by,
> And that has made all the difference.

Perestroika: Retrospect and Prospect

SINCE this book was completed in late 1988 and first published in May 1989, rapid changes have continued to occur in the Soviet Union. Eastern Europe has broken away, unfolding its own perestroika and glasnost' with breathtaking speed. The principal questions today arise from the slower pace of reform on the Soviet scene. Has it bogged down? Or is a prudent course, more appropriate to Soviet realities, being pursued? These and other questions need to be addressed now to judge perestroika's current health and to assess its future prospects.

It is necessary for this purpose to link the salient points of the preceding pages to current developments and predicaments. Several judgments, which appeared sound earlier, have been borne out by subsequent events, whereas a few have been rendered inaccurate by them.

The basic thesis of the book was that Gorbachev's strategic design was to move faster on glasnost' than on perestroika because the former was both good in itself and indirectly beneficial for perestroika. Glasnost' contributed to the momentum for arms control and reduced defense spending, thereby providing the indirect benefits of resource switching for civilian production. Glasnost' also revived détente, raising the potential for trade and technology flows from the West. Equally, in Gorbachev's calculation, well-being consisted of both freedom and bread, neither being sufficient on its own. Freedom here and now would also buy the time that the Soviet leader needed to pursue perestroika with deliberate caution.

Recent developments have only accentuated the contrasting speeds of political and economic reforms, confirming the soundness of the thesis I advanced (and contrasted with the opposite Chinese sequencing). But it is fair to say that glasnost' has accelerated even more dramatically than I anticipated. Some of the momentum undoubtedly came from events in Eastern Europe, which went far beyond any scholar's forecasts.

On the other hand, perestroika has remained on as slow a track as I predicted. I argued that the Soviet leader faced formidable bottlenecks from entrenched bureaucrats and ideological opponents, whereas the Soviet economists were also not altogether clear in their understanding of capitalist markets. But the speed of reforms has also slowed for yet another reason. An unfortunate twist has come from an unanticipated direction on this front: the increased budget deficit and the "ruble overhang" problem have created a macroeconomic crisis. As a result, the planners have time and again postponed the desired move to microeconomic efficiency via price reforms. Farms and factories need correct market signals to decide what and how much to produce, but there is so much cash in the economy that freeing prices could result in a price spiral and macroeconomic anarchy.

The current economic hardships and the perception that perestroika has bogged down are such that the outpouring of popular discontent under the banner of glasnost' now threatens to engulf perestroika's altogether slim offerings. Let me treat the current state of glasnost' and perestroika and then address the question: what should Gorbachev do now to get perestroika moving?

GLASNOST': RETROSPECT

Politics: Elections and Parties

In March 1985, Mikhail Gorbachev started with the objective of transforming Soviet socialism into an efficient economic system under the banner of the Communist Party and his continued leadership. With this end in view, the elections to the Congress of People's Deputies, extending

FIG. 10.1.   The elections with secret ballots and multiparty candidates to the Congress of People's Deputies in early 1989 and to several republican legislatures and local administrations in the winter of 1990 mark a giant stride. The fact that any and all candidates can be turned down by the voters has already made a dent in the monopoly of the Communist Party, which has a solid organization and enormous funds. Reprinted from *The Washington Post*, National Weekly Edition, April 10–16, 1989. (Copyright 1990 Buffalo News. Reprinted with permission of Universal Press Syndicate. All rights reserved.)

subsequently to the republic legislatures and local administrations, were calculated to dislodge diehard party functionaries and weaken their hold on the economy. Over time, this grand design set in motion its own dialectics: how could free elections and a single party coexist? The defeat of a few party stalwarts in the March 1989 elections to the Congress revealed the first cracks in the party's monopoly. Events in Eastern Europe, culminating in the collapse of the Berlin Wall, gave a further blow to the edifice. In the meantime, strong ethnic feelings were already rebelling against the dictates of a central government deriving power from the monopoly of the Communist Party.

Gradually, local groups have proliferated. The Popular Fronts in Armenia, Azerbaijan, and Georgia and in the Baltic republics have been the most vocal, their demands ranging from economic autonomy to cultural and linguistic identity to outright secession. At the center, the Congress of People's Deputies is blessed with a group of reform activists—450 in all (out of 2,250). This Interregional Group has neither a coherent program nor the resources to play the role of an effective opposition. On the whole, however, the members want political pluralism and free markets. With the passing away of Andrei Sakharov in December 1989, they lost a crusader commanding respect and admiration at home and abroad. The diminished moral appeal is more than offset, however, by the continuing battles, marked by ardor and expertise, of a handful of reformers on specific issues. At the same time, pluralism has brought to the fore conservative forces in the Russian heartland harking back to the glory of czarist Russia and displaying extreme traces of Russian nationalism and antisemitism. The conservative organization Pamyat' has become a forceful presence interacting with a string of right-wing journals, among them *Nash Sovremennik* (Our contemporary) and *Molodaia Gvardiia* (The young guard).

For Gorbachev, the new situation demanded a prompt and calculated response: was the time ripe now for formally acknowledging the forces of pluralism and abrogating Article 6 (incorporated in the Constitution in 1976) conferring monopoly of power to the Communist Party? At the same time, a strong central leadership was necessary so that the radicals could be placated, the conservatives subdued, and ethnic demands channeled into a constitutional process.

The response materialized at the end of a tense meeting of the Central Committee summoned for the purpose on

February 5, 1990. During the three-day debate, the conservatives warned that the country was heading toward chaos because law and order had broken down and perestroika had turned out to be empty promises and a series of mistakes: too much money, according to Yegor Ligachev, still the leading conservative in the Politburo; too little alcohol, according to Vladimir Brovikov, the ambassador to Poland. The radicals, too, warned of impending chaos because the platform lacked emphatic rejection of the very foundations of a single-party system, chief among them the party domination of the army and the KGB, the absence of intraparty grass-roots democracy, and, above all, state ownership of the means of production. Boris Yeltsin, the populist radical, complained that it was written with the left hand and the right hand. In his turn, Gorbachev promised that the party, while continuing to struggle for the role of the ruling party, would stick to a democratic process, give up legal and political advantages, offer its programs for public discussion and defend them, work with the masses, and live by their interests and needs. There was no self-denial here, merely the suggestion of a level playing field.

In the end, all 250 members of the Central Committee but one, Boris Yeltsin, voted in favor of the proposals abrogating Article 6 and recommending the formation of a presidential government with enhanced powers for the President. The final draft omitted reference to the reformist demand for changing property rights. Nor were there any attempts on Gorbachev's part to shake up the Politburo membership or discuss procedures for electing the 5,000 delegates to the forthcoming Party Congress. It was moved forward, however, to early July from October (which in turn was brought forward from its original date in the spring of 1991). Urgency, on this matter, was in the air.

No sooner was the Central Committee meeting over than the Gorbachev supporters were engaged in ensuring two outcomes: that the powers of the new presidency in the bill before the Congress be as wide as possible, and that he be elected President by the Congress of People's Deputies rather than be forced to undergo a popular election to be mandated by a vote in the Congress. On his part, Gorbachev emphasized the need for a "strong, sophisticated state" that would guarantee "civil peace and civic responsibility," arguing against a parliamentary system that could "lead into blind alleys and block all decisions" (*Izvestiia*, March 13, 1990). The debate on the issue was marked by horsetrading in the background and legislative concessions on the floor. Sergei Stankevich and Anatoly Sobchak, both first-rate professionals and sharp debaters, muscled in a few curbs on the vastly expanded powers of the presidency. As a result, the declaration of martial law or state of emergency would require the consent of the local legislature or, failing that, a two-thirds majority in the Supreme Soviet. Again, the President's veto of parliamentary legislation was made subject to an override by a two-thirds majority in the Supreme Soviet rather than by the full Congress as Gorbachev had wanted. As for Gorbachev's election to the presidency, it was managed by a narrow margin of forty-six votes in the Congress. The lobbying that delivered that precious margin was intense: Anatoly Lukianov and Yevgenii Primakov, both Gorbachev supporters, circulated rumors that the leader would resign rather than face a popular vote. Dmitri Likhachev, an octogenarian historian and gulag inmate, warned that the country would descend into civil war if a general election was called. The Latvian members of the Congress were promised a role in the negotiations for Baltic independence in exchange for their vote.

While the first President was thus elected by the Congress, his successors are to be elected by a popular vote and a simple majority of the ballots (*Pravda*, March 16, 1990). Any Soviet citizen between the ages of 35 and 65 qualifies for the job. The same person may not serve as President for more than two terms. The President can be removed by the Congress of People's Deputies only if he violates the Soviet Constitution and Soviet laws. A Presidential Council, to be appointed by the President, is to work out policy guidelines on domestic, foreign, and security issues. As a result of the new arrangements, decision making will shift from the Central Committee and the Politburo to the President and his Presidential Council. The government rather than the party will exercise power. The party, increasingly unpopular and difficult to reform, must gradually recede into the background. In the meantime, two questions arise: will the arrangements become a genuine Western-style democracy? And will they evolve into a two-party system?

As of now, the checks and balances of separately functioning executive and legislative branches of government and an independent judiciary are only sprouting. The President is too powerful and energetic, and the legislature, reacting to his agenda, rather pliant and given to oratorical excursions. As for the judiciary, it will take years to mature into an independent force. Some concessions, however, were extracted from Gorbachev in this respect, too. The President cannot remove the chief of the Supreme Court, nor can he appoint members of the Commission on Constitutional Review, which will ensure that the chief executive functions within the law: the Supreme Soviet has these prerogatives. Even so, a Bill of Rights has still to be crafted. It is doubtful if it will confer on the populace the formidable civil rights of its American counterpart. The two conceptions are miles apart. In the American version, the people decided how much liberty to hand over to the government; in the Soviet case, the process is reversed and the issue concerns the control over individual lives, which must be wrested from the government. The constitutional battles will continue well into the next century.

Will the arrangements ultimately ripen into a pluralistic political system, with two (or more) political parties, each with distinct philosophies and programs? It is too early to tell. The elections to the republic legislatures and local administrations have yet to throw up a clear pattern of political preferences. Elections of members to the Supreme Soviets of all the republics except Armenia, Azerbaijan, and Georgia have already taken place. Except in Latvia and Lithuania, where official opposition parties contested and won overwhelmingly, the Communist Party candidates were pitted against a variety of national fronts and assorted groups. While the elections were generally free with a high voter turnout, the process and results varied from place to place depending on the level of political activism and the depth of local grievances. In the Russian Republic, the Communist Party contestants won 86 percent of the seats in the legislature. But the opposition wrested control of the Moscow City Council from the Communists, and several mavericks won elsewhere—Boris Yeltsin from Sverdlovsk, *Argumenty and Fakti* editor Viktor Starkov from Moscow, and a few miners from the Kuzbass area. In the Ukraine, the popular movement Rukh captured one-third of the seats in the legislature. In Central Asia and Kazakhstan, while voter turnout was around 90 percent, there were many single-candidate constituencies dominated by Communist Party officials. They can, however, be expected to press for local issues in their dealings with the center.

What do these results suggest? Even in the politically active Slavic republics of the Ukraine and Belorussia, the opposition groups had an uphill task fighting Communist Party prerogatives arising from control of funds and the media. In the Russian Republic, the party lost Moscow but has kept control over the Supreme Soviet of the republic. The party, however, has divisions, and not all members will march to a single tune. Yeltsin's election as President of the Russian Federation in late May 1990 by a narrow margin of four votes after three rounds of voting dramatizes the split among the members of the legislature. In the Central Asian republics and Kazakhstan, the party's hold is unchanged, but, with mounting local pressures, it must assert itself vis-à-vis Moscow.

It is therefore too early for the election results to provide clear indications whether the Communist Party is on its way to a split. Such a break was avoided, more or less, at the Twenty-eighth Party Congress although Boris Yeltsin made a dramatic exit from the party, and delegates of the Democratic Platform, in all 100 (out of 4,700), announced their plan to form a new group. The proceedings of the Congress turned out to be a replay of old scenarios—tense drama, acrimonious debates from the right and Gorbachev loyalists, and Gorbachev steering the election of a new Central Committee and a refurbished Politburo. He was elected General Secretary with a decisive vote of the delegates. He also secured the election of Vladimir Ivashko, the President of the Ukrainian Republic, as the Deputy General Secretary over the candidacy of Yegor Ligachev. The Congress, prodded by Gorbachev's tireless arguments and occasional admonitions, approved glasnost' and perestroika, but its conservative membership was out of step with public aspirations for political and economic momentum. The decision making fortunately has shifted from the party to the government. In Poland, by contrast, Lech Walesa commands enough support of Solidarity rank and file to destabilize the government of Prime Minister Tadeusz Mazowiecki. Not so in the Soviet Union. Should he decide, Gorbachev can incorporate reformers in the Council of Ministers, use his emergency powers, and adopt a faster reform program.

Even if the Communist Party breaks into two factions at the Congress, it is unlikely to lead to two formal parties in the foreseeable future. Nor is it clear that the institutionalization of Soviet politics into a two-party system along the Western model is absolutely required for preventing the chaos that some political pundits have predicted. A preferred arrangement could have two features: a strong executive at the center with a popularly elected legislature, and a dominant political party capable of forming coalitions with various special-interest or local parties in the republics. For example, the framework of a strong federal government dominated by the Congress Party, forming coalitions with regional parties, under the leadership of prime ministers Nehru and Indira Gandhi, yielded by successive democratic elections for over a generation, gave India political stability and economic direction. While political arrangements cannot be transplanted, the Indian model is perhaps more relevant for the Soviet Union with its formidable economic problems and similar ethnic diversity. While the design of the political arrangements in the Soviet Union is tilted toward a strong presidency at the center, it remains to be seen if the Communist Party under Gorbachev's leadership will continue to be steered toward a left-of-center consensus and effective decision making.

The Nationalities Issue

Ethnic strife and demands for secession are threatening to break the Soviet Union apart. The deepening economic crisis partly reflects and, in turn, contributes to that possibility.

The Soviet Union presents such formidable ethnic, cultural, and linguistic diversity as to require distinct political and administrative arrangements for its governance. Its large land mass stretching 7,000 miles from the borders of Poland to the Sea of Japan has fifteen republics (fig. 10.2), each with a separate language, cultural identity, and resource base. The republics have smaller subdivisions, thirty-eight in all, demarcated for administrative convenience. Currently, this arrangement is being increasingly threatened. The autonomous region of Nagorno-Karabakh, with a Christian Armenian population, is in the republic of Moslem Azerbaijan. The autonomous region of Abkhazia, inhabited by Turkic Moslems, is locked within Christian Georgia. The Tatars would prefer to be a republic rather than an autonomous unit within the Russian Republic.

ECONOMIC AUTONOMY

Complicating the problem are the uneven endowment of resources and the growing ambitions of the republics for

Soviet Republics

FIG. 10.2. The Russian Republic dominates the Soviet Union in terms of its land area, population, and physical resources. Georgia, Armenia, and Azerbaijan are located in the Caucasus. Uzbekistan, Turkmenia, Kirghizia, and Tajikistan are the Central Asian republics. Adapted from Central Intelligence Agency, *A Comparison of the U.S. and Soviet Industrial Bases.* SOV 89-10020 (Washington, D.C., 1989).

economic autonomy. The Russian Republic is the biggest Matroyshka doll: from East to West, with a population of 147 million, it stretches the full length of the Soviet Union. It dominates the economy not only by the size of its skilled manpower but by its outputs of various products—91 percent of the country's oil, 85 percent of paper, 75 percent of natural gas, 63 percent of electricity, 60 percent of cement, 58 percent of steel, 55 percent of coal, and almost half of the wheat and meat. By itself, it not only would be fully viable; it is already a major industrial economy. The Ukraine, with a population of 52 million, is the wheat granary and a manufacturing mainstay. Belorussia, to the northwest, has fertile land, strong industry, and skilled manpower. The three Baltic republics of Lithuania, Latvia, and Estonia altogether are smaller than the city of Calcutta but are endowed with stable farming and a dairy industry, consumer goods and light manufacturing, and, by some accounts, a "bourgeois" outlook. In the southwest of the Soviet Union, the landscape changes drastically in every respect: in Kazhakhstan and the four Central Asian republics of Uzbekistan, Turkmenistan, Kirghizia, and Tajikistan, industrialization is weak, population growth rapid, the labor force largely unskilled and nonmigratory, mortality rates are higher and the political culture traditional. If resources have been diverted by the center to these peripheral outposts for reducing regional disparities, the results are not evident: Uzbekistan, Turkmenistan, and Tajikistan produce 90 percent of the cotton but lack a textile industry; Kazhakhstan is a substantial producer of wheat and coal but has remained essentially a raw material supplier. Finally, in the Caucasus, Georgia produces fruits, vegetables, and tea in abundance and has an energetic, freewheeling culture. Armenia and Azerbaijan have a smattering of manufacturing, but further potential is thwarted by specific factors: oil production in Azerbaijan has been declining, and material supplies to Armenia are thwarted by Azerbaijani blockades of railways at the border.

This unevenness of resources among the republics has fueled demands for greater autonomy from Moscow in economic matters, with the affluent republics also wanting to retain more and share less with the less prosperous ones. At issue also is greater autonomy in questions such as pollution control and a larger role for the local language. As for the Baltic republics, the situation has rapidly escalated to one of independence, raising an altogether different class of "decolonization" problems for Gorbachev.

The economic arrangements between the center and the republics are becoming increasingly untenable. Currently, almost all revenues via taxes and profits of state-owned enterprises flow into the central coffers. The center owns almost all productive assets. The republics and local administrations receive part of the taxes and allocations from the central budget for administering social services such as health care and education. As a result of the perestroika reforms, they have received formal authority to expand consumer goods production in their areas, improve their supplies, set up cooperative and consulting firms, and gear trade and infrastructure to local needs. By and large, matching funds to carry out these activities have followed. The republics have acquired a bigger say in the central planning of investment decisions on their territory.

But the current arrangements continue assigning a peripheral role to the republics and local authorities in investment, production, and financial activities. The planners decide where new factories will be located. Even trivial decisions flow from the top: "How long will some Ivan Petrovich in office No. 421 continue deciding whether a public toilet should be built in a Lithuanian city whose name he cannot even pronounce?" asked the rector of Vilnius State University at a roundtable discussion (*Pravda*, November 2, 1988). The ministries decide which enterprises will receive funding for expansion of major capacities from central funds. Above all, the prices of various items continue to be set by Goskomtsen (the State Price Committee) in Moscow.

It is difficult to work out the net balance of gains and losses that follows from these arrangements. But almost every republic complains that it is exploited by Moscow. Most vociferous in this regard are the Central Asian cotton growers, among them Turkmenistan and Uzbekistan. With explosive birth and high infant mortality rates, they resemble developing country rural areas. Families in Turkmenistan have ten or more children whereas Russian families have one or two (*Pravda*, November 2, 1988). The infant mortality rate in Turkmenistan is 58.2 per 1,000 births, in sharp contrast to 11.6 in Lithuania (ibid.). Uzbek children spend at least a third of their school time working on cotton plantations (*Kommunist* 15, October 1988). Labor is plentiful and wages are at subsistence levels. The low standard of living creates a sense of exploitation by the more prosperous regions, arousing complaints such as that the purchase price of cotton for shipment to the textile mills in the European parts of the land is too low. Among other complainants are the oil producers in western Siberia, who argue that they supply oil everywhere at half the world prices.

A change in the current arrangements is therefore a pressing issue for Gorbachev. How has he responded?

At one extreme, he has faced the Baltic republics, which began with demands for total local control of all resources including land, air, and water. They wanted private property, a separate currency, and a free hand in managing foreign economic relations.* But surely such strident economic demands could not be realized without political sovereignty. The battles with Moscow had to be joined on the political front. The Popular Fronts, which began as grassroots, unofficial (*neformal'ny*) movements, finally emerged as opposition parties, ultimately gaining control of the local legislatures in the February 1990 elections in Lithuania and Latvia. From the start, the escalating process was unique in that it was fueled by the forced annexation of the Baltic republics in 1940 by the Soviet Union on the basis of the Molotov-Ribbentrop pact and the ultimate goal of secession that it inspired.

Far more moderate positions have been expressed by others, especially the Central Asian republics. They desire greater economic autonomy but insist that the problem of resource transfer from the "haves" to the "have-nots" must not be lost sight of. Formally, the issue boils down to the definition of a self-financing unit: should it be an en-

* On being elected President of the Russian Republic in early June 1990, Yeltsin echoed similar demands for the Russian Republic. Not to be outdone, Gorbachev announced immediately thereafter that in the proposed federation, the republics could sign a treaty with Moscow as autonomous and equal partners. Later, at the Twenty-eighth Party Congress, the Politburo was expanded to include the first secretaries of the Communist Parties of the fifteen republics. Such a pluralistic arrangement was designed to soften the dominance, in the Politburo, of conservatives from the Russian Republic.

terprise or a republic? That is, should republics be self-sufficient (like enterprises), or should they share with one another? As early as September 1988, a group of economists and sociologists from Estonia had proposed (*Kommunist* 15, October 1988) that the unit of "economic accountability" should be the republic or regions within it, implying no sharing by the republics. At the Nineteenth Party Conference in June 1988, the issue was vigorously debated. The surplus republics, among them the Ukraine, Belorussia, Moldavia, Georgia, the Baltic republics, and several autonomous regions of the Russian Republic, were naturally in favor of such an approach: a prospering republic should be entitled to maintain its own accounts and plow back its profits for the betterment of its own population. It may, of course, choose to *lend* its surplus funds to a needy republic. On the other hand, the deficit republics were naturally opposed to this idea of "every tub on its bottom" since it would deprive them of the automatic transfer of funds from a common pool under central direction.

Gorbachev's initial response to the emerging debate provided several guidelines (*Pravda*, November 28, 1988). The tunnel vision of nonsharing republics threatened not only perestroika but the Union itself. Moreover, the Soviet Constitution was binding on all the republics; local laws that violated it were therefore invalid. True, the republics and other territories must have a greater voice in economic decision making. But land and mineral deposits, which were a common property of the Soviet people, could not be transferred to a republic.

Gorbachev also stressed that the country was linked by networks of rail and air transport, electric power and fuel supplies, and deliveries of metals and machines. How could all this be effectively separated? On the other hand, light industry, trade and services, and social welfare activities could be passed on to the jurisdiction of local bodies. The economic basis of the Union would then rest on ownership and management of heavy industry, transport, and communications by the center.* Nevertheless, the local authorities would acquire rights to tax the units in their territory. Local revenues would be enlarged by transfers from the central budget. A common currency to be managed by a central bank would prevail. Enterprises would increasingly be allowed to enter into arrangements with foreign partners, but Vneshekonombank (the State Bank for Foreign Economic Affairs) would continue monitoring and regulating foreign exchange earnings and use until the ruble became fully convertible.

In short, the economic decentralization, to be incorporated in the ongoing legislation, can be expected to allow for a common currency, central management of foreign exchange earnings, and, at the very least, central control of industry profits as the "milk cow" for redistribution by the state. Enterprises, however, will increasingly be freed from control by central ministries in their decisions to invest and innovate. While heavy industry, transport, and communication units may eventually be converted into joint-stock companies, central ownership is likely to persist via a dominant share in their equity. The ensuing fiscal battles between the center and the periphery in the coming years will, in all likelihood, be reminiscent of medieval jousting rather than a polo match.

THE LANGUAGE ISSUE

The language issue is as much a matter of promoting economic well-being as of cultural identity. While there are fifteen major languages, some are less equal than others. Russian is the dominant language not only by virtue of being the language of the largest nationality but also because it is the means of communication in administration and the courts. It is the language of higher education, of science and technology, of the professions and skilled oc-

---

* As these units are converted into joint-stock companies according to the provisions of the Property Law (discussed below), the center will be left with the powers to influence the pricing of major items and to impose corporate and other taxes.

cupations, and of culture. One must know it well in order to advance and prosper.

While the rest of the major languages are important in local use and education in the schools, the many dialects must struggle to survive. For example, there are only 800,000 people who speak Chechenian in the autonomous republic of Chechen-Ingush in the Russian Republic. Each group wants to be nourished under glasnost'. The issue is further complicated by the presence of sizable minority groups in each republic. Kazakhstan has 41 percent Russian, 30 percent Kazakh, 6 percent Ukrainian, and 2 percent Tatar settlers ("Where is the expert skillful enough to divide up Kazakhstan?" Gorbachev asked in a conversation with members of the Young Communist League, *Pravda*, April 12, 1990). In all, about 60 million people live outside the republic of their nationality (ibid.).

The problem of the domination of Russian is discussed as energetically as the virus of centralized decision making in the economy. At the June Party Conference, minority language representatives complained about the practice of reserving higher-level jobs—for example, engineers and foremen—and certain industrial branches, such as machine building, for those who could speak Russian. Thus, Estonians have expressed outrage at Russian settlers in well-paid, high-tech jobs in Estonia (*Kommunist* 15, October 1988). As a result of such migration into Estonia, the proportion of Estonians in the population has dropped from 90 percent in 1940 to 62 percent currently (*Izvestiia*, February 12, 1988). Again, construction workers, mostly Russians, are ahead in the line for housing allocations, which are denied to Estonians who study music and art (*Sovetskaia Estonia*, December 18, 1987). The result of this linguistic hegemony is that the knowledge and value of non-Russian languages have declined even among native speakers. At the same time, Russian-language chauvinism has degenerated into "intellectual apartheid" by the Russian minority. Long-term Russian settlers in Estonia do not know Estonian nor do they care (ibid.).

Several republics have now passed laws adopting the local language as the official language of the republic. The Moldavian legislature has not only legislated in favor of Moldavian but also declared that Latin rather than Cyrillic, enforced by Stalin, be adopted as the script. While republic languages will evidently be the means of communication in local administration, courts, education, and industry, it is hoped that Russian will play that role in the conduct of affairs between republics and with the center. Needless to say, the transition will not be achieved overnight. There are few textbooks for school children in Uzbek. The domination of Russian in the life of the land has been complete. Legal statutes, industrial-technological manuals, and textbooks for instruction, especially at the higher levels, are in Russian. Typewriters with characters in the local language are hard to find. The telegraph offices in Georgia must decipher telegrams that have Georgian words but are transmitted in Russian characters; neither a Georgian nor a Russian can unravel the message (*Pravda*, November 2, 1988).

While local languages and cultures will gradually establish a foothold, the minorities in the republics will face the choice of having to assimilate or leave. The Popular Fronts in the republics have been formed essentially along ethnic-linguistic lines. Non-Latvians in Latvia complained recently that the draft law on language did not include their views (*Pravda*, March 1, 1989). In February 1989, the Presidium of the Latvian Council of Ministers considered measures with ominous consequences for minorities (*Sovetskaia Latvia*, February 15, 1989): as a result, admission to technical and vocational institutions would be restricted to permanent residents of the republic or temporary trainees from outside. Only permanent residents and people with continuous residence in Latvia for at least ten years may be included in waiting lists for better housing. There are similar restrictions on the sale of private housing. Enterprises are to contribute to a fund for developing housing and infrastructure for every additional nonlocal employee (including Latvian workers from distant areas). Since Rus-

sians are an important minority in almost every republic
except the Russian Republic, such laws would in effect
discriminate against them. A new breed of dissidents will
surely emerge.

DEMANDS FOR POLLUTION CONTROL

Across all republics, there are now vociferous demands
for protecting the local environment and physical resources. Private enterprise in market economies, geared to
profit making, cannot be expected to concern itself with
environmental damage. The state must step in to resolve
the conflict between private benefit and social costs. Since
measures to protect the environment result from government initiative and action, many thought at first that the
record would be better in socialist economies where
growth takes place under state direction. But state action
on the environment has typically resulted from public
opinion and pressure, which were altogether ineffectual in
the socialist countries until glasnost' took hold. The socialist record on the environment therefore was abysmal
rather than exemplary.

The situation is changing, but the issue now arises as a
republic versus Moscow problem. Since the central planners and ministries decide the location of industries, each
republic currently blames Moscow for its pollution problems. The problem is not that the central planners discriminate deliberately against any republic when its environment is polluted. Rather, the problem is that they simply
do not care about the environmental impact of their economic decisions. Thus, nuclear hazards arise in the western parts of the country because the nuclear power plants
happen to be located there. Industrial pollution follows the
factories, which are generally set up in areas where there
is infrastructure or raw materials. Such pollution is uni-
formly serious in parts of the Ukraine, around Lake Baikal,
and in western Siberia, which is the favored location for
the petrochemical industry.

The catalyst for pollution control came with the Chernobyl nuclear power plant accident in the Ukraine on

April 26, 1986. The local administrations and people continue battling its aftereffects in neighboring Belorussia too. Equally serious is the drying up of the Aral Sea in Central Asia: the waters of the rivers flowing into the sea have been diverted to irrigate the cotton crops in the region. The heavy use of fertilizers and the resulting toxic residues have contributed to the high infant mortality rates in the region. Soviet media continue to give graphic details about the dying sea and public outrage. Environmental lobbies in Kazakhstan have also begun protesting that nuclear tests have been conducted routinely in remote areas of the republic without concern for local sentiment.

All in all, with the economic-autonomy, language, and pollution issues fusing into a formidable set of problems on the "nationalities" question, it is doubtful if the old practice of central control of economic decision making can continue any longer. While factories and service industries will develop under local initiative and entrepreneurial drive at varying pace, the large industrial units under central control will have to function with increased local autonomy. Skilled jobs in these factories will have to pass on to the natives. Their profits will have to be shared for local use. A mountain of legislation on the division of economic decision making, on revenue sharing, and on dispute settlement will come up gradually on the agenda of the Supreme Soviet. Its actual implementation will witness continuing give-and-take and frequent legislative updates with pressures coming from public protests.

In the meantime, this slow but inevitable process has been upstaged by escalating events in the Baltic republics.

THE BALTIC REPUBLICS

On March 11, 1990, in an all-night session, the Lithuanian Supreme Soviet passed a law declaring itself independent from the Soviet Union. The timing was calculated to preempt the forthcoming legislation on the common framework of procedures, under discussion by the Supreme Soviet, allowing republics to secede from the Union.

As can be expected, the now-legislated Soviet procedures are designed to prolong such exits (*Pravda*, April 7, 1990). The first step is a referendum in which 66 percent of the republic population must vote in favor of secession. Next, the details of issues such as the division of centrally owned assets (including military installations), the rights of minorities, and the cost of resettling them elsewhere must be sorted out in a period of up to five years. The secession must be finally approved by the Congress of People's Deputies.

The Lithuanian Supreme Soviet reacted by insisting that Lithuania was forcibly annexed so the legislation from Moscow was irrelevant. In the meantime, Soviet tanks and armored vehicles rolled into Vilnius, reviving memories of Budapest (in 1956) and Prague (in 1968). The Communist Party office and a printing press in Vilnius were occupied by central emissaries. Foreign reporters were ordered out of Vilnius, and the economic sanctions against Lithuania escalated from reduced deliveries of oil and gas to other raw materials. These events were followed by the adoption of similar but less confrontational legislation by the Latvian and Estonian Supreme Soviets. The leaders of the three republics met subsequently to discuss details of common economic arrangements. The continuing developments give a new meaning to the allegorical opening of the Pandora's box. In the meantime, what lessons can be drawn from these events?

First, the right of Lithuania as well as Estonia and Latvia to be independent was recognized by everyone. A resolution passed by the Congress of People's Deputies acknowledged that the Baltic republics were illegally annexed to Soviet territory. The next logical step was to establish the procedure for letting them go. Inside the Soviet Union and outside, the Baltic situation was generally recognized as unique: the United States, for instance, had never officially recognized these republics as part of the Soviet Union. As a result, Baltic aspirations escalated into secession demands with impetuous haste. The peaceful rallies with hands linked for miles on end, the stirring melodies of the national anthems, the resounding election victory of the Popular Front, Sajudi, in the winter 1990 elections to the Lithuanian legislature not only exhibited a highly developed, almost non-Russian political culture but also put a stamp of legitimacy on their demands in the eyes of all beholders. If ever there was a land deserving freedom, little Lithuania was it. The leadership calculated that Lithuania would be recognized as an independent state by the United States, perhaps followed by Western Europe and the rest of the world.

From the moral point of view, it was an impeccable case. But, by and large, Gorbachev's claims proved more compelling. U.S. recognition of independent Lithuania would not only hasten similar demands for secession by other republics and divert Gorbachev's energies from the demanding tasks of perestroika but threaten East-West détente, the arms control negotiations, the continuing progress on German reunification, and the steady momentum of events in Eastern Europe toward democratic pluralism and market-type arrangements, which promised the eventual departure of Soviet troops. The Lithuanian Supreme Soviet was advised by all and sundry to suspend the independence declaration as a basis of negotiating with Gorbachev. On his part, Gorbachev failed to extract a promise of a speedy ratification by the U.S. Senate of the Trade Treaty signed by the two presidents at the June 1990 Washington summit.

The first lesson from the episode is that even the Baltic republics cannot expect to be recognized as independent states unless they stick to the timetable set by the center.*

---

* On the eve of his departure for the Washington summit, Gorbachev offered independence to Lithuania at the end of two years if only the Lithuanian Supreme Soviet suspended the independence legislation. Since then, there have been continuing signs of mutual accommodation by Gorbachev and the Baltic leaders on the procedural issue of Baltic independence. The economic sanctions against Lithuania were lifted at the end of June 1990 in return for a 100-day freeze on the independence legislation by the Lithuanian Supreme Soviet.

They will, at best, get moral support. If elsewhere nationalist demands get hasty and even violent, as they may, the dispatch of Soviet troops and tanks will be construed as necessary for maintaining law and order in Soviet territory.

The second lesson relates to the economic aspects of the secession issue. President Gorbachev came up with a bill of $33 billion as the price of Lithuanian secession. It is difficult to know how he arrived at this number. Perhaps it is the cost of the factories, the public housing, and the military installations owned by the ministries in Moscow. But such numbers are inherently subject to debate, as students of colonialism well know. Thus, the Lithuanians feel they have been exploited by being forced to sell their consumer goods and electronic products at cheap prices in the rest of the country. Moscow claims that Lithuania has received fuel, metals, and materials at subsidized prices. Calculating the costs and benefits of colonizing Lithuania can be an economist's nightmare.

When passions have cooled, the Baltic republics may find it to their advantage to sell their products in Soviet markets in exchange for Soviet oil, gas, and other materials. They may find it hard to penetrate Western European markets even if, as independent states, they ultimately become members of the European Community. There would be saving of transport costs on selling items in the Soviet market, which, for better or for worse, will always remain next door. For the Soviet Union, too, it would be profitable at the margin to continue to sell fuel via existing pipelines. The exchange can take place in hard currency at market prices. It would be foolhardy to give up historical ties that can be adapted to be mutually profitable. This important lesson is especially true in the short run.

The economic embargo on Lithuania has brought home to the other republics the dangers of abruptly severing political and economic ties with the rest of the country. Except perhaps the Ukraine, they are in a similar predicament. The Georgians produce abundant fruits, vegetables, tea, and wine, but again, like the Baltic republics, they depend on subsidized deliveries of fuel and materials, among them grain. There is an added dimension to the possible disruption from precipitous severing of economic ties, at least in the short run. A consequence of centralized planning has been that many factories in one republic receive materials from a single supplier in another. The major producer of ice-cream cones is located in Lithuania. The soap factory in Yerevan in Armenia, one of the biggest in the country, receives almost all its tallow from Moldavia. Such accentuated dependence by one republic on others makes adventurism, in the shape of extreme demands for self-sufficiency and autonomy, less sustainable.

WILL THE UNION FALL APART?

From a historical perspective, the Soviet Union has caught up with the Western world and reached the ultimate phase of nation building on the basis of voluntary consent of its constituent units. Will it hold together?

The Soviet Union, like other countries of comparable size, has grown via conquests. The relevant question in its current historical phase of nation building is whether the conquered lands consider themselves part of a nation. California and New Mexico are the fruits of conquest, but they feel sufficiently assimilated to want to continue in the American republic. In their case, past conquests have become current realities and ultimately an emotional bond. Such transition is taking place now in the Soviet Union after a long process of territorial expansion, stretching out to the non–Slavic territories under the czars, and their subsequent consolidation after the revolution. Czar Alexander I (1801–1825) not only conquered most of the Caucasus, including Christian Georgia, then an autonomous state, and Moslem Azerbaijan, but also grabbed a slice of Bessarabia, currently in Moldavia, from the Turks. He was followed by Czar Nicholas I (1825–1855), who conquered parts of present-day Armenia from the Turks in 1828. The legendary conquests of Russian frontiersmen extended, during the reign of Czar Alexander II (1855–1881), to the

FIG. 10.3. Controlling ethnic passions and nationalities' demands would test any leader's parenting skills to the utmost. It is, however, a chore that cannot be passed on to someone else. Gorbachev's latest pronouncement in mid-June 1990 offers the republics the choice to sign a treaty as "sovereign" partners. Reprinted from *The Washington Post*, National Weekly Edition, February 12–18, 1990. (Copyright 1990 Universal Press Syndicate. Reprinted with permission. All rights reserved.)

rugged wilderness of Central Asia. The lands of Kazakhstan, Kirghizia, Tajikistan, Uzbekistan, and Turkmenistan were captured then. All these territories were
already part of the Czarist Empire for at least half a century
at the time of the Bolshevik Revolution. The next phase
under Stalin was marked less by conquests and more by
the redrawing of internal boundaries: the Baltic states were
annexed in 1940, western Ukraine was carved out of Polish
territory in 1945, and part of Rumania was combined with
Moldavia in 1944. But, by and large, central control of
existing territories became the goal of policy, replacing
outright conquest of new territories. There was, in consequence, neither much autonomy nor republicanism in the
units that were christened "Republic" or "Autonomous"
this or that in the process.

Now that autonomy is within the grasp of the republics,
would they want to stay in the Union? Wouldn't the memories of having lived together for at least a century ultimately prevail? Clearly, the variety of languages and reli-
gions pulls them apart. Seventy years of communism have
failed to provide an ideological or cultural bond; nor has it
weakened the religious fervor of the Moslem masses or the
Slavophil longings of the ordinary Russians. Can one look
for a parallel and lessons elsewhere? Hardly. The Soviet
scene compares unfavorably even with India, which is diverse and so poor. In 1947, the British left a country unified by a single administration and a basic railway network. But there was already much more. For the majority
of people, the memories go back to more than two millen-
nia of unifying philosophical and cultural traditions and a
common religion. Despite the formation of the Indian
states along linguistic lines, and buffeted still by separatist
demands, the federal union has held together.

The Soviet Union misses the glue that comes from memories of history nourished by the emotional bond of religion or the unifying impulse of a common culture. By all
accounts, the Russian Republic, with a population of 147

million, has a common cultural, ethnic identity. This identity cannot, however, be extended to include other republics. Thus, for instance, whatever affinity the Ukrainians and Belorussians feel with the Russians as Slavs is undercut by historical animosities and linguistic differences.

But perhaps not all hope is lost. Rather than secede, a republic may settle for a flexible arrangement within the Union out of strategic economic considerations. As I have noted, they are locked in close economic ties, which could be made mutually acceptable. The Russian Republic supplies fuel, metals, and materials at less than market prices to the rest, but it also receives consumer goods and agricultural items—grain from the Ukraine, cotton from Central Asia—at favorable prices. Besides, twenty-six million Russians, who are generally in high-income managerial and skilled jobs outside the Russian Republic, are perceived as beneficiaries, if not agents, of a dictatorial economic regime. The market can correct the pricing imbalance, but interrepublic egalitarianism will require an active federal government promoting "affirmative action" to benefit the disadvantaged majorities and extending "foreign aid" to the underdeveloped republics.

Again, noneconomic considerations may carry weight. It is not clear that each non-Russian republic wants to walk out. The least likely to consider secession is Armenia: the central government provides protection from the Turks to the west and the Azerbaijanis to the east, both traditional enemies. Both Kirghizia and Kazakhstan border China on the east. If Soviet-Chinese relations continue to improve, China will be a benign neighbor everywhere along the common border and have no incentive to support an extremist secessionist movement in either republic. The Azerbaijani extremists may dream of a bigger homeland by uniting with their five million Shi'ite kin in the northern parts of neighboring Iran. Whatever the shape of Soviet-Iranian relations, Iran is not ready to part with its northern territory. In view of its own territorial compulsions, therefore, Iran is unlikely to support an extremist secessionist movement in Azerbaijan.

It is not clear that the predominantly Moslem republics will want to exit en masse from the Union. They are not a homogeneous religious group. The Uzbeks and Kirghiz are predominantly Sunni Moslems whereas the Azerbaijanis are Shi'ite. Again, within each republic, there are interethnic feuds: in June 1989, almost a hundred Meshketian Turks, a relatively prosperous group, died in fights with Uzbeks. By and large, these republics subsist on a thin margin with high unemployment. With greater freedoms, ethnic harmony has become fragile—the Dushanbe riots in Tajikistan in February 1989 were prompted by rumors of housing allotments to Armenian migrants. The bloody fights between the Kirghiz and Uzbek populations in early June 1990 started with allocations of land in Kirghizia. Even in relatively prosperous Georgia, relations between the Georgians and the minority groups of Abkhazians and Ossetians are not altogether harmonious. The federal government may still be perceived as a benign arbiter and necessary protector.

A serious jolt to the Union may come, however, from the Ukraine and Belorussia in the west. These two, along with the Russian Republic, have about 70 percent of the population, almost all of its heavy industry, and a staggering share of natural and mineral resources. Will the cultural and linguistic diversity pull them apart? Or will the potential for shared economic benefits of staying together in a truly autonomous federal arrangement prevail? Nationalism ultimately is an emotional force, and rational calculations have an uphill task in countering it. Gorbachev appealed to the Lithuanians in January 1990, saying, "How do you know? You have not lived in a federation." It was a pragmatist's approach of "If you tried it, maybe you would like it." But by that time, Lithuania had already reached a point of no return. So also Latvia and Estonia. The future Soviet map will have to be drawn without the

Baltic republics. As for the rest, the process of preserving the territories in a genuine federation will continue in the years ahead. There is no guarantee that it will succeed. But it is not certain that the federation will disintegrate either. The outcome will depend on two factors.

First, a strong central leadership functioning under glasnost' with a mix of firmness and flexibility may succeed in keeping the nationality demands on a constitutional track of give-and-take. That is the best hope of channeling the process away from extremist options. Extreme demands will certainly occur from time to time. Thus, for instance, before the Soviet Army marched into Baku on January 19, 1990, the Popular Front leadership had passed into the hands of extremists. The movement, which began under the inspiration of Baku intellectuals of diverse beliefs, among them Russians, Armenians, Jews, and Azerbaijanis, had been pressed into extremist postures and tactics under pressure from the unemployed proletariat migrating into the city from the rural areas and neighboring Armenia. Even more destabilizing would be the resurgence of conservative forces in the Russian Republic under Pamyat's banner. Such extremism may be contained, however, in an environment of free debate, peaceful rallies, and frequent elections.

The new ability of people to travel to and fro, and the indulgence of legitimate ethnic and religious aspirations, are also important. It is helpful that Moldavians are allowed to visit across the border in Rumania. The mass visits by Azerbaijanis to northern Iran in February 1990 may have helped take the edge off violent displays of ethnic and religious aspirations. The Moslems are now going on pilgrimage to Mecca. Finally—who, indeed, would have thought of it!—even the Old and New Testaments are now to be filmed with Finnish collaboration in cartoons.

Second, friendly relations with neighboring countries, for example, China and Iran, may prove as critical as involving local leaders and populations in the process of working out a looser, freer arrangement among nationalities. Such support, as was provided by the Bush administration and several European governments despite the dispatch of troops and the economic blockade of Lithuania, may not always materialize, but the policy of good-neighborliness will give dividends with progress on the nationalities problem as with the prospects of perestroika.

Indeed, resolving the nationalities issue and keeping perestroika alive are closely linked. If the economy were to perform better, the demands of the nationalities, occasionally turning to violence, could perhaps be contained: there might be less unrest and more resources to satisfy the backward republics. So how is perestroika doing?

PERESTROIKA: HOW FAR?

Not only have there been no compelling breakthroughs in the economy, but the lines appear to be longer, more shelves are empty, and the forecasts are gloomier. The 1989 scorecard of the economy has the same old litany— shortages, poor quality, wages far outstripping the small productivity gains. The official estimate of the 1989 GNP growth rate, based on conventional Soviet estimating procedures, was 3 percent (*Pravda*, January 28, 1990). The Central Intelligence Agency, which employs the more reliable market-economy method, has put the GNP growth rate at 1.4 percent (U.S. Congress, 1990, table C-4).*

All of this suggests, in any event, that perestroika has either broken down or been counterproductive. But neither conclusion is warranted. Definite institutional changes, which are preconditions for full-scale market and price reforms, have by now been laboriously legislated. Also, a few policy-cum-institutional changes, in sectors such as agriculture, industry, and foreign trade, have cre-

---

* Anders Aslund (1990a, 23), having proclaimed a growth rate of –5 percent for 1989, has forecast it at –10 percent for 1990. But his pronouncements, like those of some Soviet writers, are not grounded in any scientific methodology.

ated the pressures and the necessary political support without which serious reform can be neither begun nor successfully implemented. But the pace and sequencing of the steps that Gorbachev must now take toward price reform and markets remains an issue that divides economists in the Soviet Union and abroad.

Before I discuss these questions, let me turn to the institutional and policy changes that have begun to materialize under perestroika in different sectors of the economy. In discussing these changes and whether they indicate progress toward the market, I will follow the sectoral classification adopted in this book.

Industry

The major sectors of Soviet heavy industry, among them fuel, electricity, steel, and machine building, had anemic performance in 1989. Consumer goods, with a growth rate of 4.8 percent in official sources, outpaced heavy industry growth of 0.7 percent. The official estimate of the industrial growth rate was 1.7 percent in contrast to the Central Intelligence Agency estimate of a mere 0.2 percent (U.S. Congress, 1990, table C-4).

The year 1989 thus marked a decisive shift of Soviet industry from its traditional emphasis on heavy industry. The more critical question is whether the plan is giving way to the market in Soviet industry. Hardly. The enterprises continue to be dominated by the plan and by the ministries in their production and investment decisions. In the new framework of the Law of the State Enterprise, factories are to be allowed to produce items contracted for sale to other factories and to purchase materials for the purpose from other than the state suppliers. But, by all accounts, ministries have continued assigning compulsory state orders to factories. Indeed, state orders have been restored in consumer goods industries with a view to ensuring supplies of essential consumer goods in the 1991–1995 Plan announced by Prime Minister Ryzhkov in December 1989.* Again, the ministries have continued to make major investment decisions. Enterprises still deposit about 8 percent of their profits with ministries for financing branch investments and technical programs (*Pravda,* October 3, 1989). These contributions are on top of tax payments, from profits, to the central budget.†

There are a few silver linings, however. While production remains largely geared to compulsory state orders, wholesale trade in materials has reached an impressive 25 percent of the total (*The Economist,* March 15, 1990, 29). Moreover, all units in the state sector now operate on full cost-accountability and face the risk of being shut down if they make losses. As a result, the number of enterprises showing losses declined to one out of ten in 1988 (*Pravda,* January 22, 1989). Finally, enterprise leasing is proceeding apace: by the end of 1989, 1,332 industrial enterprises, 731 construction organizations, and 988 retail trade outlets were operating on leasing principles (*Pravda,* January 28, 1990).

But the old questions still persist: How can factories be rescued from ministerial controls, be motivated by profits, and start making production and investment decisions? How can proper incentives be created for the purpose? By now, the answers are familiar as well. There must be market signals and a genuine pursuit of profits based on ownership of assets. While Gorbachev postponed price re-

---

* A *New York Times* editorial on December 18, 1989, cited my view that the Ryzhkov plan's proposed recentralization in the consumer goods sector was a crisis management step necessary until the infrastructure for price reform was set up (rather than a *permanent* regress from price reform). The question whether it was a backward step from the framework presented by Leonid Abalkin, the deputy prime minister, in November 1989 is distinct though related. While some, such as Aslund (1990b), suggest that it was, I do not think this is a correct inference, as I argue below; the "Ryzhkov-Abalkin differences" are grossly exaggerated.

† In the new tax proposals before the Supreme Soviet, the enterprise tax, reaching a total of 60 percent of profits, is to consist of two parts: a fixed tax of 35 percent for the central budget, and the remaining to be decided by the republics (*Pravda,* October 3, 1989).

forms once again in April 1990, he won a significant political and ideological battle on the critical property rights issue in early March.

The Property Law was passed by the Supreme Soviet on March 6, 1990 (*Pravda*, March 10, 1990). Perhaps the most categorical clause in this law is that land, water, mineral, and timber resources belong to the people in a territory (Article 20). In effect, all natural resources, including land, belong to the state. But, for all else, Section III of the law states the procedures for converting state units into non-state enterprises. Different possibilities are envisaged and permitted. The state units can be changed into joint-stock companies with stock ownership by citizens. They can be leased to a worker collective or a cooperative or a partnership, which may then decide to buy them.

Interestingly, the law forbids exploitation of man by man or the alienation of a person from the means of production. This concession to socialist concerns, however, is likely to be pro forma, designed to win a consensus through an ideological compromise. It is unlikely to turn into a Trojan horse, impeding the privatization process and the ability to run these nonstate enterprises efficiently. For similar reasons, the law does not use the term "private property."

Finally, regarding the issue of ownership by foreigners, the law now permits mixed ownership, including joint ventures between Soviet and foreign legal entities and citizens.

The law thus provides an enormous potential for privatization. But the process will be pell-mell at best. It will also be slow. Many problems will arise in practice. How are the plants and factories to be valued? Where is the private wealth that can be used to buy these units? The creation of a functioning stock market itself would be a slow process.

In practice, many state units will remain state-owned. For most of them, the transition will involve intermediate arrangements under which they may be leased and run efficiently by their own workers and management or by other efficient enterprises.

In the meantime, therefore, the essential element of reform will have to be focused on the fact that not all state enterprises will become joint-stock companies, cooperatives, or partnerships. Indeed, some will continue to be publicly owned in the foreseeable future. It is important that these units operate efficiently in an environment of "hard" budget constraints in which market prices prevail and rival producers compete. With the winds of privatization blowing all across Eastern Europe, state enterprises, which have never been subjected to the discipline of the market, are being singled out as the root of all evil. They have remained safe havens of bureaucratic administering, overstaffing, and trade union activism. As leases, cooperatives, and joint-stock companies start appearing in Soviet industry, the resulting competitive pressures should help slap the state units into shape.

Agriculture

Despite widespread assertions to the contrary, Soviet grain performance has not deteriorated. The 1989 grain output increased by 16 million tons to 211 million tons. More to the point, grain yield rose to an all-time high of 1.88 tons per hectare (U.S. Department of Agriculture, 1990, 35), exceeding 1.85 tons in 1978 when grain output reached an all-time high of 237 million tons. Also, the average annual variability of output has declined significantly in the past four years in relation to the earlier years.

In the meantime, the problem of institutional reforms and price incentives to secure better *production* performance has been only partially attacked and remains to be addressed further. In addition, there is the new situation of emptying shelves in state stores across the country. This is a problem of *distribution*—which I will discuss in depth below—and paradoxically owes its emergence to the gradually emerging success of the limited perestroika in agriculture.

What has perestroika amounted to in agriculture? The traditional technological approach to increasing agricultural production, taking the institutions and prices as "given," has of course been pursued as before. Thus, the planners have assigned substantial funds to the agricultural sector for new rail lines, covered wagons, improved grain elevators and regional storage facilities, better harvesting machines, and mixed-feed mills (*Pravda*, June 23, 1989). But the institutional reforms, designed to usher in the incentives without which farmers do not provide the necessary "tender loving care" in farming, were still missing. These were unveiled by Gorbachev as his new agrarian policy at a party Central Committee meeting in March 1989 proposing a variety of arrangements for getting a handle on the situation. The Soviet state and collective farms, 50,000 in all, were to continue. They would be encouraged to reorganize themselves as clusters of households that, in turn, would lease land from the farm. An individual family, too, would be free to move out and lease land and equipment.

Gorbachev's proposed program contrasted with the more ambitious one implemented by Deng Xiaoping in China. The Chinese experimented briefly with leases within the framework of the communes, beginning in 1978. But although farm output increased substantially, the Chinese swiftly dissolved communes during 1982 and 1983. The decollectivization by 1984 led to elimination of production quotas by 1985 and the abolition of the state procurement monopoly. The farmers were free to produce and sell grain at prices set by the government. But grain prices were not remunerative. The farmers therefore turned to other cash crops, even to rural industries, where higher profits could be made. The result: average grain output between 1985 and 1988 was below the 1984 level.

Why did Gorbachev choose the less radical route of proposing state and collective farms existing side by side with household and collective leases? He undoubtedly confronts a more complex ideological landscape. Over the decades, the farms have become important symbols of the socialist regime. As Ligachev remarked in Omsk prior to the Central Committee meeting in March 1989, when faced with a query on the decollectivization of just the unprofitable farms, "It was not for this that we established Soviet power." Ligachev also protested that a breakup of the unviable farms, by eliminating state support, would leave the households to fend for themselves. This would reduce them to destitution, unacceptable under socialism. Gorbachev's riposte was that the state could not continue such support endlessly.

The lease system, with the farms in place, offers a workable compromise. It enables the productive farmers to strike out on their own, with prospects of prospering on their leaseholds, while the farm becomes increasingly unviable with only the uneconomic elements gradually left within. Instead of Chinese-style dissolution, Gorbachev would appear to have chosen the less divisive, if slower, Darwinian process of disintegration of the unviable farms. He evidently opted for a reform path that was more suited to the Soviet political and economic circumstances.

It was, however, almost a year before the law to implement the scheme was passed by the Supreme Soviet (*Izvestiia*, March 7, 1990). As a result of this law, local soviets are now authorized to give land to citizens for life, and to organizations, among them kolkhozes, sovkhozes, and cooperatives, for permanent tenure (*vladenie*) (Articles 5 and 6). (They can also give land to individuals and organizations for industrial and other uses.) These rights of tenure are authenticated in a State Deed whose details are defined by the union republics (Article 8). The soviets can also lease land temporarily to individuals, farms, or cooperatives. The lease can be converted into a tenure by mutual agreement of the parties (Article 7). The tenure holder would pay a tax whereas the leaseholder would pay a rent, each set by the union or autonomous republics (Article 12). State and other agencies are forbidden to interfere in the activities of individuals and farms (Article 18). The tenure holder can pass on the tenure to his heirs but may not divide the plot (Article 25). Evidently, the lawmakers are not ready to allow land transactions via outright sale. Only permanent tenures and leases are allowed. At the same time, individuals who are denied tenure can appeal to a court of law (Article 26). Members who choose to leave a farm are entitled to a plot that is an average share of the total value of the farm set in the land survey (Article 26).

Like the Property Law, the new Land Legislation has enormous potential for freeing state and collective farms from state and party control and gradually ushering individual farming into the Soviet countryside. But this will unfold in the future. In the view of Soviet economists, expressed in a Supreme Soviet opinion poll, private farming will account for no more than 5 to 10 percent of the arable land by 1995 (*Izvestiia*, February 16, 1990).

Currently, however, the ongoing perestroika reforms have already led to a set of changes with major implications in regard to state procurement of food and distribution in state stores. These changes include self-financing and cost accounting on the farms, providing increased freedom to the farms to manage their own affairs. As a result, farms have been exercising their new freedoms to select inputs and output composition, and in other ways. Thus, they have begun shifting grain area to more profitable activities. Some have even switched to forage crops, bringing down grain plantings to 112.3 million hectares in 1989 (U.S. Department of Agriculture, 1990, 35), which is as low as in 1954 (soon thereafter the Virgin Lands program went into full swing under Khrushchev). Subsidies to farms on their purchases of industrial inputs, among them machines and fertilizers, were steadily reduced in 1988 and 1989 (ibid., 12), and farms are currently using fewer fertilizers and pesticides. They are also increasingly exercising their right to reject deliveries of farm machines (ibid., 13).

But the most striking and, from the planners' point of view, the most damaging exercise of free choice by the farms has been in the area of grain deliveries to state procurement agencies. The state managed to procure only 59 million tons of grain from the farms in 1989, 27.3 million tons less than planned. State procurement of grain, at its highest in 1986, has been declining despite offers of steadily increasing prices to the farms on their deliveries. Farms have simply looked at the prices offered by the state for grain sales to it and turned away to more profitable sales elsewhere. The problem is that state procurement, traditionally treated as the only alternative* in preperestroika days, is no longer the only game in town, and if it yields less, that is, has elements of an implicit tax, the players simply move to another game.

The traditional state procurement also operated as an implicit tax in another way. Most farms need mixed feed (for rearing livestock), which is processed in state units. Indeed, the state buys grain for making flour (for bread and pasta) and livestock feed. But, according to the U.S. Department of Agriculture (1989b, 23), farms in the Ukraine selling grain in procurement for 97 rubles (per ton) must pay roughly 150 rubles for the mixed feed they buy, a deal that inexorably pushes them toward on-farm processing. The farms have therefore been increasingly converting grain into feed and channeling it into meat-producing units of their choice. While most poultry and hogs are processed in large state units, beef is produced in dispersed facilities located near or on farms and by the farm households themselves. The emerging possibilities of selling grain and meat in nonofficial markets also make procurement (at lower prices) increasingly less effective.

The result of the drastic decline in state procurement of grain has been reduced mixed-feed production and lower meat supplies in state stores. The grain deficit resulting from failing procurement has been largely filled by im-

* The state purchases or "contractual" deliveries, on a quota and "above-quota" basis, were not in the nature of formal procurement *levies*, though the quotas were always met "voluntarily" earlier (failure to fulfill them meant demotion or early retirement for the farm chairman). Now, the voluntary nature of the system has become truly pertinent.

ported grain. (In the past decade, according to the U.S. Department of Agriculture [1989a, 9], the total of domestic procurement and imports has remained more or less stable at 106 million tons.) However, this partial picture of lagging procurement and insufficient livestock feed production and meat supplies in the state sector does not mean an overall decline in livestock feed and meat production. Official meat production in 1989 at 20 million tons marks a continuing gain of output over 15 million tons in 1985. The U.S. Department of Agriculture (1990, 42) estimates of livestock feed for 1989 also show an improvement over 1988. The problem is therefore as much one of distribution as of production, akin to the "marketed surplus" problem in the early literature on the Soviet economy.

The resulting headache for Gorbachev's planners is that, while more meat is available in the economy, the urban housewife is unable to get it in state shops at the artificially low prices. How will the planners deal with these consequences of the farms exercising supply choices under perestroika's loosening reins? Ultimately, the market must be left free to decide the price of everything from grain to livestock feed to meat. It may still be necessary, during the transition, to make limited rations of meat and bread available at subsidized prices.* The budgetary cost of financing the required subsidy will have to be met by taxing the farms explicitly rather than via the now-defunct practice of an implicit tax. In his acceptance speech on being elected President, Gorbachev mentioned the possibility of an agricultural tax: he was on the right track.

Cooperatives

The cooperatives have proven to be the most energetic segment of the economy. While serving as effective channels for entrepreneurial energies and means of employ-

---

* This question, and a proposal to introduce a "dual-pricing" solution, are taken up in the last section.

ment, they now provide services and light industry products. On the other hand, they have been criticized as "exploiters" and "speculators," buying materials at controlled prices and selling their products and services at "exorbitant" prices. Their normal profit-seeking behavior, which underlies the market economy, has evoked strong reactions: public protest has occasionally spilled into destruction of cooperative property, factory managers have complained about the loss of skilled workers, and trade unions have protested the favorable treatment of cooperatives vis-à-vis state enterprises.

The government has reacted by enacting escalating restrictions on cooperative activity. The Council of Ministers' Resolution of December 29, 1988 (*Izvestiia*, December 31, 1988), prohibits cooperatives from making vodka, weapons, and drugs, publishing books, making films, establishing schools, dealing in foreign currency, and providing major medical services. A few other activities are to be allowed only on the basis of contracts with enterprises and state organizations. More legislation is on the way: the draft law on income tax, to be applied to incomes from cooperative and private activity, has proposed progressive tax rates rising to 50 percent on monthly incomes above 1,500 rubles. The current flat tax rate of 13 percent on all monthly earnings above 100 rubles is to be discontinued (*Pravda*, April 15, 1989).* Another draft law before the Supreme Soviet would authorize local administrations to issue cooperative licenses only for the activities that they consider important. Cooperatives will be allowed to have only one account with a bank in the area in which they are registered; all full-time employees of a cooperative will have to be accepted as members with full rights rather

---

* While the average monthly earnings of state workers range from 240 to 260 rubles and those of collective farm workers are 200 rubles, cooperative workers are estimated to be earning 500 to 600 rubles (*Izvestiia*, April 3, 1990). The new tax rates, beginning July 1, 1990, are approximately 14 percent on a monthly income of 1,000 rubles, 20 percent on an income of 1,500 rubles, 33 percent on an income of 3,000 rubles, and rise to 45 percent on an income of 5,000 rubles (*Izvestiia*, May 11, 1990).

than "hired hands"; and cooperative members will not be allowed to escape liabilities for the debts they have incurred (*Izvestiia*, April 9, 1990).

During a May visit to a Moscow textile factory, broadcast on the evening news, Prime Minister Ryzhkov declared (in reaction to a worker's demand that cooperatives should not be allowed) that they should be regulated rather than banned. Despite the stifling dose of regulations proposed by Ryzhkov and generally approved by the Supreme Soviet, cooperatives continue to multiply, currently employing five million people.

Foreign Trade and Joint Ventures

While Soviet trade accounts with hard currency and socialist trading partners showed small negative balances in 1989, for the first time since 1976, there were no dramatic changes in the pattern of exports and imports. Oil has continued being the major hard-currency earner, accounting for about half of the foreign exchange earnings. In 1986 and 1987, consumer goods imports were slashed to make way for machines to promote capital stock renovation; they have now been reinstated. Throughout the period, substantial grain imports normally have been financed with cash payments, but, more recently, short-term credits have been used. While Soviet hard-currency debt has climbed to $47 billion (U.S. Congress, 1990, 14), the ratio of annual debt repayment obligations to export earnings at 23 percent (*Financial Market Trends*, February 1990, 26) is still respectable.

While the traditional trade pattern has not altered drastically and the debt situation is still manageable, the new trading arrangements under perestroika have brought to the surface new tensions. Trade in major commodities, among them oil and raw material exports and grain imports, is still managed by the FTOs. These items cover up to 80 percent of the trade turnover. As for the rest, exporters deposit their earnings in accounts with Vneshekonombank, and importers, while forbidden to incur net foreign exchange liabilities, nonetheless have greater freedom to buy from abroad than ever before and then, having done so, to approach the bank for hard-currency requirements. Despite the restrictions, the temptation to "import now, pay later" has proven difficult to forgo and liabilities have piled up, so that the bank has either delayed or refused foreign exchange clearance for imports. There have been recent reports of delayed payments to the tune of at least $1 billion for purchases of German products, Japanese steel, Australian wool, and U.S. grain. These liabilities are being met by the sale of gold and the offer of gold as collateral to raise Western bank credits. Soviet gold stocks of 2,000 metric tons are currently worth about $28 billion and get replenished by 250 to 300 tons annually.

The problem of "overimporting" would of course disappear if the exchange rate were flexible: the exchange rate would adjust to bring the supply and demand for foreign exchange into equality. With the current fixed exchange rate of the ruble, the excess of imports over exports must be paid out of hard-currency reserves (including gold) or by capital inflow or by credits. The Soviet Union has naturally adopted a sensible policy option and taken advantage of the recent access to short-term credits by acquiring them to the maximum. But short of full exchange rate flexibility (which has other consequences), a less ambitious way of getting a handle on the external payments problem is to ensure that permission to use foreign exchange is given to importers only within the limits defined by foreign exchange availabilities, by instituting an exchange control or an import control regime or both, as is the case in many developing countries. At the same time, since the attendant rationing implies a scarcity premium on foreign exchange, it is sensible also to consider auctions of foreign exchange. This has begun, and the (limited number of) auctions have begun chipping away at Vneshekonombank's traditional preference for allocations of hard currency. The successive auctions have registered a sharp decline in the value of the ruble, reaching a rock-bottom rate of twenty-one rubles to the dollar on May 22, 1990. (The special rate for tourists is set at six rubles and seventy kopecks per dollar, whereas officially, the dollar exchanges for sixty-seven kopecks.) The importers may well use their hard-earned foreign exchange to import "nonessential" items for which there is a lucrative market. So be it, since the distinction between essentials and nonessentials is itself for the most part a bureaucratic creation rather than reflective of economic rationality.

As for the inflow of investment and technology via joint ventures, it is but a trickle despite the liberal provisions permitting foreign partners much leeway in running these ventures. As of January 1, 1990, altogether 1,274 joint ventures of all kinds (mostly export-import businesses) were registered in the Soviet Union (*Pravda*, January 28, 1990). But barely 6 percent had brought investment and technology. A few giants, such as Combustion Engineering in oil technology and McDonald's, do carry substantial equity so that, in terms of investment, the contribution of foreign investors substantially exceeds 6 percent of all deals signed.

In effect, a bipolar pattern is emerging in joint venture activity. At one extreme are a number of small companies supplying essential services to foreigners and engaging in export-import activity. They rely on minimum investment and technology for their presence on Soviet territory. While their scavenging brings to the fore new items in the trade arena, they are not popular with Soviet planners who see them incorrectly as bringing little investment and hence no permanent gain to the economy. Even so, some of these small activists have acquired a firm foothold. They are viable because, with a minimum investment of their own, they earn hard currency, and, having guaranteed for themselves an acceptable return, they expand their ruble operations. A successful example is AlphaGraphics Printshops of the Future, which runs modern, high-tech, quick-printing centers in the Soviet Union (*New York Times*, Business Section, May 6, 1990, 21).

At the other extreme are the big players who, after prolonged negotiations, have decided to settle in for the long haul without being permitted to convert their ruble profits directly into dollars. They bring their equipment (for which they arrange the financing) and supply the technology. Occasionally, the current operations also involve hard-currency expenses. For example, on each sale of a hamburger, the Moscow McDonald's incurs foreign-exchange costs on the plastic containers that are manufactured abroad. How is repatriation of profits handled then? Two joint venture arrangements throw light on the different arrangements for repatriating profits. The American Trade Consortium, consisting of an oil corporation (Chevron), an agricultural company (Archer-Daniels-Midland), a photography-products manufacturer (Eastman Kodak), a consumer-products maker (Johnson & Johnson), and a food and tobacco giant (RJR Nabisco), has been negotiating about twenty-five joint ventures with the Soviet Foreign Economic Consortium. Chevron has already signed a protocol with the Soviet Ministry of Oil and Gas Industry to undertake a feasibility study of developing the huge Tengiz oil field in the northeastern Caspian Sea region. The rate at which the partners in the consortium can convert their ruble profits into dollars is tied to the dollar earnings that Chevron helps promote from its participation in the Soviet oil industry. On the other hand, McDonald's will be allowed to charge (and retain for profit repatriation) dollar payments for hamburger sales in another restaurant, which will start operating soon.

The dual pattern thus involves many small companies who have ensured foreign-exchange earnings for themselves and a few large corporations who have worked out special arrangements to repatriate profits through barter or similar arrangements tied to their earning foreign exchange for the Soviet Union.* There is a minimal role currently for middle-level companies who would step in only if they are allowed to repatriate their profits directly. That must await Soviet ability to earn hard currency by diversi-

---

* The question of repatriation of ruble profits is tricky enough. Equally difficult can be the problem of recovering dollars expended in importing components and materials from abroad to keep the plant going.

fying and pushing exports in Western markets. In the meantime, as leases, partnerships, and joint-stock companies appear in Soviet manufacturing, the licensing arrangements (as opposed to joint ventures) may provide opportunities for profitable collaborations. Currently, potential collaborators are deterred as much by the prohibition on converting ruble profits directly into hard currency as by the procedural nightmares of doing business with Soviet partners. The interminable delays, the continuing layers of state agencies, the multiplicity of forms, and unclear contracts test the patience and pioneering spirit of the most daring individuals. The bureaucratic procedures still remain to be substantially streamlined if foreign investors are to be seduced in a world economy where the competition for foreign investment is getting more intense.

On to Price Reform?

What, in conclusion, is perestroika's contribution in various sectors of the economy? From industry to foreign trade, there are signs that the economic agents want to make choices and exercise initiatives. In industry, factories want to deal increasingly with clients—buyers and sellers—of their choice and switch to higher-priced products. In agriculture, farms are reacting to the unfavorable terms of trade—to low prices of grain paid by the state in exchange for high prices of feed grain charged by the state—by producing their own feed and using it themselves or selling it to the meat producer of their choice, and the cooperatives have continued expanding. Finally, there is, of late, excess demand for imports, stimulating the price rationing of foreign exchange via auctions rather than direct allocation by the central bank. These are remarkable positive signs.

But the question arises: will the Soviet planners react constructively to these pressures and let markets and prices roll in? So far, despite occasional pronouncements implying that such moves were imminent—as when Gorbachev became President *extraordinaire* in March 1990 and put the economy on top of his agenda—a decisive program involving a shift to flexible prices has not materialized. An important reason underlying this hesitation, not evident until around 1988, was the appearance in the economy of new, *macroeconomic* problems. Unless these problems were resolved first, the shift to flexible prices for securing *microeconomic* efficiency gains could prove inflationary, perhaps hyperinflationary, and require sudden monetary and fiscal brakes resulting in massive disruption, unemployment, and the possible demise of perestroika. Let me elaborate.

MACROECONOMIC DISEQUILIBRIUM VERSUS MICROECONOMIC EFFICIENCY: FIRST THINGS FIRST

When Gorbachev became General Secretary in March 1985, the economic "crisis" that he inherited (and which I discussed in this book) was not macroeconomic but microeconomic. The Soviet growth rate had fallen sharply, reflecting sluggish advances in technology and diminishing returns to investment. Farms and factories needed incentives to produce, innovate, and invest in an environment of efficiently functioning markets if the economy was to be turned around. But by 1988, for reasons discussed in Desai (1989), macroeconomic disequilibrium had become an issue of importance rivaling that of efficiency via market prices.

Different Types of Shortages

How does one distinguish macroeconomic from microeconomic disequilibrium? At the outset, a distinction must be made between localized (or sectoral) shortages and generalized (or economywide) shortages.

When one walks down a Moscow street and sees a long line for sugar, or reads about backlogs of orders for automobiles, these may indicate merely that the suppliers have underproduced these specific commodities (while presumably overproducing others). The market demand for these items, at the "administered" fixed prices, exceeds their supply. Such localized shortages at fixed prices have long been known to occur under central planning. At fixed prices and centrally determined production quantities, supply and demand frequently do not match. Desired goods are often scarce, while undesirable goods pile up. There is, in economic jargon, "microdisequilibrium." The situation can be remedied if production quotas are removed and prices are allowed to move freely. Producers and consumers would adjust their supplies and demands to these market signals with some prices moving up and others moving down. With such adjustments in relative prices, the overall price level may not change much.

In a situation of "macrodisequilibrium," by contrast, there are generalized shortages. At the fixed prices, many goods are in scarce supply. The shortages may be truly economywide and extend to all sectors, including investment goods. The economy is generally overheated, but the universal price rigidity leads to widespread lines and empty shelves for consumer goods, and backed-up orders for investment goods.

Currently, generalized shortages appear to have materialized in the Soviet consumer goods markets. It is not possible to track down shortages for machines because, unlike bread lines, one does not see investors waiting in line for machine tools or diesel engines. Normally, such excess demand takes the form of backed-up orders. Data on such backlogs of orders are routinely collected in most Western economies but are not yet available from Soviet sources. By contrast, shortages of consumer goods are in full public view. Not only have lines become longer, but an ever-increasing number of items have moved out of retail trade and begun to be distributed via coupons, special orders, barter arrangements among factories, and invitations to fairs (*Izvestiia*, March 29, 1989).

The flip side of this phenomenon of consumer goods shortages is that those who wish to spend money and buy more goods (at fixed prices) are unable to do so; there is frustrated, pent-up, excess demand. If prices were allowed to rise, inflation would result. Prices would go up and absorb the desired increment in spending. With fixed prices, there is instead "repressed inflation." Shelves are empty, lines are long, and those who wish to buy more are instead compelled to save.

The Ruble Overhang and the Budget Deficit

Over the years, the Soviet people have accumulated their savings in the form of extremely liquid assets. The state has owned almost all means of production, with the result that the public has not had the option to invest in enterprise stocks. While some cooperative housing has developed, a few well-to-do own dachas, and rural dwellers have homesteads in the villages, the overwhelming stock of residential apartments has not been available for private ownership until recently. Very few are interested in owning government bonds that have a yield of less than 3 percent. The public has therefore been constrained to keep savings in the form of cash or bank deposits. These bank deposits total a hefty 337.7 billion rubles (*Pravda*, January 28, 1990), approximately equaling the annual sales of consumer goods and services in state and cooperative stores. As for cash at home, the estimates range from 90 billion rubles (*The Economist*, June 17, 1989, 16) to 240 billion rubles (Central Intelligence Agency, 1989, 7).

By and large, therefore, the Soviet public holds extremely liquid assets that can be readily shifted into purchasing goods and services. If inflationary pressures begin to arise and expectations of future price increases or shortages are intensified, this ruble overhang can result in a massive increase of spending, seriously compounding the inflationary problem.

The "stock" phenomenon of the ruble overhang therefore acquires a threatening character when the situation becomes inflationary. The inflationary pressure itself can originate, as it has under Gorbachev, from an increased budget deficit that is not matched and "financed" by corresponding private saving. In the Soviet context of controlled prices, the inflationary pressure will result not in increased prices, but in excess demand for goods and long lines. This failure of consumers to find goods with which to satisfy their desired consumption amounts to what economists call "forced saving." The combination of an inflationary budget deficit and the ruble overhang would then represent a serious problem. This, I would argue, is what the Soviet economic situation currently amounts to.

The Situation before Perestroika

At the outset, however, consider the situation with regard to the ruble overhang, the budget deficit, the involuntary savings by Soviet citizens, and consumer goods shortages when Gorbachev became General Secretary in March 1985. It seems reasonable to say that there were localized consumer goods shortages as always, but there was little compelling evidence of generalized consumer goods shortages and involuntary saving by Soviet households.

At its peak in the late 1970s, the household savings of bank deposits, barely 5 percent of personal disposable income, were not excessive in comparison to other countries (Pickersgill, 1976, 139–47); however, since these deposits were heavily concentrated in a few households, with 3 percent of the households holding 50 percent of these deposits, these individuals might have been forced to save. The stock of past savings was held in the form of liquid assets, that is, cash and bank deposits. The budget deficit was a source of dissaving, but not in any dramatic fashion: it had averaged roughly 2 percent of GNP during 1981–1985.

But by 1988, macroeconomic disequilibrium had become a critical issue. What happened?

Macroeconomic Disequilibrium under Perestroika: 1985 and Thereafter

After 1985, reduced revenues led to a substantial budget deficit. Wages drifted up in excess of productivity increases. A sharp increase in investment implied a significant reduction in the normal growth of consumer goods supplies. The combination of these three factors contributed to unprecedented growth of involuntary savings, with the demand for consumer goods outstripping their supply.

BUDGET DEFICITS

The budget deficit, 2 percent of GNP on average during 1981–1985, jumped sharply to 6 percent in 1986 and came close to 8 percent in 1987 and 1988 (Central Intelligence Agency, 1988, x). The planned deficit of 100 billion rubles for 1989 would lead to a deficit of 11 percent (Bergson, 1989, A10).

The problem was more with revenues than with outlays. The official data do not reveal a sharp departure in the growth of total outlays and their key components in 1985–1987 from their growth in 1981–1984. Thus the outlays allotted to the three main categories—the national economy, social and cultural expenditures, and defense—were steady at 55 to 57 percent, 33 percent, and 5 percent respectively in both periods.

The budget revenues, unlike budget outlays, grew steadily only up to 1985. They have remained at the 1985 level since. Turnover tax revenues declined substantially from 1984 to 1987, mainly because alcohol tax receipts declined from 44 billion rubles in 1984 to about 32 billion rubles in 1987 (*Narkhoz*, 1984, 574; 1987, 589–90). The anti-alcohol campaign, spearheaded by a cut in state production of liquor, had all too predictable results: an undiminished propensity to booze, flourishing bootlegging, and a decline in state revenues. Yet another casualty in the post-1985 years was the revenue from trade taxes. The decline in world oil prices cut state revenue from oil exports by narrowing the gap (accruing to the treasury) between foreign and domestic prices. The cutback in imports of consumer goods in 1986 and 1987 also caused diminished revenues from taxes on these items. These shortfalls were not offset by increased accruals to the budget from other sources.

WAGES AND PRODUCTIVITY

After 1985, most enterprises abandoned their restraint on wage increases. Average monthly cash earnings of workers and office employees grew at the average annual rate of 2.4 percent during 1981–1985, but these were more than matched by the growth of labor productivity at 3.1 percent. By contrast, 1986–1988 saw these monthly cash earnings increase annually at 4.5 percent, exceeding a growth of labor productivity of 3.8 percent (*Pravda*, January 22, 1989). The gap widened in 1989, with the former having grown by a staggering 13 percent and the latter by 2.3 percent (*Pravda*, January 28, 1990).

This reversal of the earlier, prudent exercise of an effective "incomes policy" was accommodated by the extension of short-term credits by Gosbank to the enterprises. The wage inflation, in turn, seems to have arisen from the new, if limited, reforms under which enterprises have been allowed to pay higher wages to "more productive" workers. Traditionally, a sort of incomes policy was in place because enterprises were assigned production targets and a matching wage fund to pay the work force. Now enterprises can vary employee earnings. According to Academician Aganbegyan (*Pravda*, February 6, 1989), the payments to workers based on unfinished construction-and-installation work went out of control. At the same time, the need to use monetary policy to control the resulting inflation was not fully appreciated.

FROM CONSUMPTION TO INVESTMENT IN PRODUCTION

While incomes grew and productivity lagged, the composition of output in the economy also shifted. Consumer goods yielded to a larger share of investment goods (for example, steel pipes) in total production. While gross fixed investment in the economy, in 1984 rubles, had grown annually at an average rate of 3.5 percent during 1981–

1985, it had jumped by 8.3 percent in 1986, 5.7 percent in 1987, and 4.8 percent in 1988 (U.S. Congress, 1989, 42). The higher growth rates of the perestroika period, though declining from year to year, were driven by calls for *uskorenie* (acceleration) and conquests of new technologies. By contrast, the per capita annual growth rate of consumption, in 1982 established prices, already low at 0.8 percent during 1981–1985, had actually declined by 1.5 percent in 1986, and barely grew in 1987 and 1988 (ibid.).

The shift away from consumption to investment goods in national production and availability was perhaps the unintended consequence of the leadership's decision at the Twenty-seventh Party Congress to turn the economy around. It was occurring just as the other factors, such as higher wages, were intensifying consumer demand. Thus the imbalance between supply and demand became wider.

CONSEQUENCES

The net result would have been involuntary savings matching the excess demand for consumer goods at the fixed prices. Soviet prices, though, are not altogether rigid. The illegal second economy allowed for some effective price flexibility (especially in services) even before the advent of perestroika. Again, the device of introducing "new" products (on which higher prices are allowed) can become a vehicle for smuggling in price rises. Excess demand can therefore be absorbed somewhat by such price increases.

In fact, Soviet sources indicate that retail prices of consumer goods rose at 1.7 percent annually during 1986 and 1987, twice the average rate of 0.9 percent for 1981–1985 (*Narkhoz*, various years). According to Central Intelligence Agency estimates, the figures may have been higher: 3.4 percent for 1986 and 2.1 percent for 1981–1985 (Central Intelligence Agency, 1988, 5), and 6 percent for 1989 (U.S. Congress, 1990, 7). Official Soviet sources report, in a rare display of glasnost', that the price index of produce in the collective farm (*kolkhoz*) markets (where anything from potatoes to pork is sold freely) rose at 2.6 percent in 1981–1985 but much more rapidly, at 9.4 percent, in 1986. According to Goskomtsen, the rise in prices of consumer goods in 1989, including repressed inflation, was 7.5 percent. The comparable Gosplan (State Planning Committee) estimate was 10.5 percent (U.S. Congress, 1990, 7).

But the main result of this imbalance between consumer demand and supply, with generally rigid prices, was to create involuntary savings and shortages. Household savings increased sharply. During 1981–1984, they averaged 11.4 billion rubles annually. They rose to 24 billion in 1987 and were 13 billion in the first half of 1988 (Central Intelligence Agency, 1988, 7). It is entirely possible that this increase reflected involuntary savings. As for shortages, they became everybody's favorite theme—from forthright complaints to Gorbachev at the famous encounter in Krasnoyarsk to complaints and cartoons in newspapers. Economists, among them Vasilii Sel'yunin (*Sotsiialisticheskaia industriia*, April 6, 1989) and Nikolai Shmelev, predicted chaos if shortages were not removed—the former urging speedy reforms and the latter, massive imports. While admitting the urgency of remedial action, Gorbachev hastened to reassure himself that the Soviet people would not reject perestroika just because the stores were short of commodities. The standard of living, he declared, included not only material items but also dignity and freedom, the gifts of glasnost'.

In the meantime, shortages intensified. Dishoarding of some of the stock of rubles, in anticipation of a price reform and higher prices, may well have put added pressure on consumer goods markets. Nikolai Shmelev recently remarked that a Moscow friend had stocked up a seven years' supply of detergent. Shortages were reported even of matches and salt (*The Economist*, June 17, 1989, 16). Tea, generally imported from soft-currency earnings and hence readily available, also became scarce.

While the current shortages are macroeconomic in origin, they are exacerbated by distributional problems. For example, meat is hard to find in state stores although over-all meat production and supplies have edged forward: the empty shelves, as I argued earlier, also reflect failing procurement of grain (for conversion into livestock feed in state units) at implicit-tax-inclusive prices.* Again, there are other distributional problems, reflecting the nationalities problems discussed earlier and the resulting interruptions of supplies by some republics. Thus, Kirghizia and Kazakhstan have passed laws prohibiting enterprises from shipping items outside the republic: consumer goods from the former and above-quota outputs of consumer items from the latter (*Izvestiia*, February 24, 1990). Occasionally, supplies earmarked for specific destinations have been sabotaged en route, accentuating specific shortages and adding to the situation of generalized shortages. But there is no denying that the overall macroeconomic situation constitutes a major problem compounding Gorbachev's economic problems and complicating his move to price reform.

Possible Policy Measures to Restore Macroeconomic Equilibrium

What can be done, then, to rescue a microeconomic program of price flexibility from the macroeconomic straitjacket in which it has come to be imprisoned? The solution must have three parts: curtailing the budget deficit, activating monetary policy, and addressing the ruble overhang.

---

* Pure macroeconomic shortages with too much money chasing too few goods have to be distinguished from a situation where such shortages are aggravated by distribution problems as with the reduced availability of meat in state stores. The latter can be redressed by policy measures such as an agricultural land or income tax enabling the state to purchase grain in rural markets at market prices (for conversion into livestock feed in state processing units) for subsequent production and distribution of meat at the desired, lower prices in state stores. Applying monetary brakes and creating unemployment to deal with this problem would be like prescribing open-heart surgery for a hernia.

REDUCING THE BUDGET DEFICIT

Consider outlays first.

(1) Defense. An obvious candidate for direct reduction of outlays is defense spending. Such a cutback reduces the deficit directly and contributes significantly to the solution of the problem of inadequate voluntary savings in the economy by requiring the rest of the economy to save less. The cutback lowers the deficit indirectly by leading to a shift in production from defense to consumer goods, thereby raising revenues from turnover taxes. In Soviet practice, these taxes are heavily concentrated on consumer goods.

These cuts will contribute significantly to the solution of the problem of inadequate voluntary savings in the economy by reducing budget deficits. The rest of the economy must save less if the government cuts its deficit (i.e., dissaving).

(2) Investment. Like reduced defense outlays, a rollback in budget-financed investment would directly lower the budget deficit, divert resources to the production of consumer goods, and indirectly ease the budget deficit via larger turnover tax revenues from the increased production of consumer goods. But while lowering defense outlays yields a permanent gain, lowering investment reduces future growth potential. If the planners had postponed the proposed Tyumen petrochemical complex in western Siberia and instead diverted the resources to set up shoe, soap, and textile factories, the switch would have raised current consumption and government revenues from taxes on these items but reduced the economy's future potential for expanding these very same industries—petrochemicals are an important raw material for soap, shoes, and textiles. By contrast, a permanent shift of existing defense capacities to the production of consumer durables would not cut the economy's future growth prospects.

(3) Consumer subsidies. The prices that Soviet consumers pay on their purchases of meat, milk, butter, bread,

and so forth have not been raised from the 1962 levels fixed under Khrushchev. In the meantime, the state has been paying increasing prices to the producers of these items since 1965. The difference is financed by the state budget. Until May 1990, when bread prices were slated to triple by July 1,* Gorbachev had avoided any cuts in these consumer subsidies. In fact, subsidies on food items were slated to increase in 1989, reaching 19 percent of the budget.

The reluctance to reduce these subsidies had an arguable rationale. If a large enough dent could be made in the deficit through major cuts in defense and minor cuts in investment, and through increased revenues, then it was unwise to cut subsidies on key consumer goods such as meat, bread, and milk. Aside from being politically unpopular, these cuts would be regressive. The political upheavals in Third World countries that often attend the implementation of International Monetary Fund austerity measures could not have escaped Gorbachev's attention.

Next consider budget revenues.

(4) Importing consumer goods. The import of consumer goods results in revenues from the taxes levied on their sale. In addition, if any imports are credit-financed, they have a greater beneficial effect on excess spending: they increase total goods availability without adding to overall income and hence expenditures. The domestic production of these items, by contrast, would result in additional wage payments, which would add to the current pressures to consume more.

(5) Producing consumer goods. Shifting production from other goods to consumer goods also helps by adding more revenue from turnover taxes. But it cannot have the added beneficial effect that credit-financed imports can have on the problem of excess demand. For in a situation of full

---

* At the same time, the procurement price paid by the state for grain was raised, on average, by 50 percent (*Izvestiia*, May 8, 1990), so the net reduction in subsidy may be negligible.

employment, if consumer goods increase in supply, other goods must correspondingly diminish in supply. The reduction in excess demand in consumer goods markets would then be matched by increase in excess demand in markets for other goods.

ACTIVATING MONETARY POLICY

The diminished control over enterprise wages, production, and investments also requires that Soviet authorities now learn to use monetary policy to regulate the demand for investment goods and the working capital required for inventories and wage payments.

Gosbank should no longer be advancing funds to enterprises as in the past, when they were provided almost routinely to lubricate enterprise activity. Now, with greater enterprise freedom in the works, such an "accommodating" monetary policy could have serious inflationary consequences. The intention of the Law of State Enterprise is to encourage enterprises to economize on labor and material costs and make profits. This goal cannot be realized if enterprises continue to get funds virtually cost-free from Gosbank and to use them for excessive wage payments and material stockpiles.

Soviet banking in general needs to be organized along commercial principles. In the new arrangements already in place, the banks (like all state units) have been put under the rule of full cost-accounting. They should also be allowed to earn a reasonable rate of return on their loan operations. Another issue here is the need for an effective instrument for curbing enterprise borrowing. In the traditional practice of *kontrol'rublyom*, a local official of a Gosbank branch would more often than not approve the request for funds because he could be held responsible if the output plan of the enterprise failed due to shortage of funds. Now, he must be able to regulate borrowing by using the interest rate, varied by Gosbank authorities. Unfortunately, such a step has been slow in coming.

SOLVING THE RUBLE OVERHANG

These measures will address the "flow" problem of excess spending, and the repressed inflation associated with it, currently plaguing the Soviet economy.* The "stock" problem of the substantial ruble overhang also needs to be contained to avoid massive dishoarding and consequent inflationary pressures when prices are let loose. But how?

Higher interest rates would help by converting some of the involuntary saving into voluntary saving. The promise of increased consumer durables in the foreseeable future—through schemes such as signing on for cars and other durables for future delivery with current downpayments—is another possibility.

A solid opportunity for soaking up the Soviet public's excess liquidity also lies in the possibility of letting Soviet citizens buy the apartments they currently rent from the state. Housing is the most substantial of the assets the state has come to acquire in the Soviet economy, going well beyond the Marxist ideology that the means of production should be owned by the state. In the process, the state has intensified official interference in people's lives, taking over the burden of managing housing properties. If the state cannot run factories properly, it cannot have any special aptitude for managing housing either. The plans to privatize housing thus would not merely make a big dent on the ruble overhang, but should also create more efficient management and maintenance of the stock of housing.

CURRENCY REFORM

Can the Soviet planners consider introducing a currency reform as an effective way of soaking up excessive cash in

---

* The need for an incomes policy that would link wages to productivity, at least during the transition to a flexible-price economy, is discussed below. Its main role is to put less burden on monetary policy in achieving macroeconomic equilibrium and hence creating less unemployment, *ceteris paribus*.

the economy? A look back in history on this issue is of interest.

An earlier version, arbitrary and unexpected, was introduced under Stalin on December 14, 1947. Its target was the peasantry, which had amassed cash from the high prices of food in the *kolkhoz* markets during the Second World War. Except for bank accounts of 3,000 rubles or less (which could be converted into new rubles at the rate of one-to-one), all cash holdings were to be exchanged at the rate of one new ruble for ten old rubles. The small savings of the urban proletariat were treated less severely than the large cash holdings of the peasants. There were no compensating adjustments in either wages or prices, so the reform amounted to outright confiscation.

A far less severe plan was adopted in the South during the American Civil War to deal with the unprecedented rise in prices from October 1861 to March 1864. "On February 17, 1864, the Confederate Congress enacted a currency reform. All existing currency and call certificates, except one-, two-, and five-dollar bills could be converted, dollar for dollar, into 4 per cent bonds until April 1, 1864. The notes still outstanding on April 1 were to be exchanged for new issues at the rate of three for two. With this one law, one-third of the South's cash was erased. . . . In May 1864, the currency reform took hold, and the stock of money was reduced. Dramatically, the general price index dropped. This price decline took place in spite of invading Union armies, the impending military defeat, the reduction in foreign trade, the disorganized government, and the low morale of the Confederate army. Reducing the stocks of money had a more significant effect on prices than these powerful forces" (Lerner, 1956, 172).

There are therefore alternative ways to implement a currency reform that would essentially reduce the ruble overhang problem. It is unlikely that the Stalinist version, which is more transparently a confiscation of past savings, can play under today's glasnost', especially when Gorbachev has no clear political mandate for major surgery on the economy. The Confederate Congress model, while also drastic, seems less so because it offers a choice of conversion into a (low-yielding) asset. A partial freeze on cash in bank deposits is yet another alternative.

The principal reason for going along the route of currency reform would be the inevitable slowness of policies such as privatization of apartment ownership and the creation of a stock market with equity trading. It also allows the planners to reduce the costs of measures such as offers of lucrative interest rates on bonds so that involuntary cash holdings can be converted into voluntary assets. The ultimate transition to substantive price flexibility therefore is likely to involve some version of currency reform, though (for obvious reasons) a public admission of the desirability or inevitability of such a policy is unlikely to come before the policy itself.

Measures Adopted for Restoring Macroeconomic Equilibrium

The preceding analysis shows how the microeconomic disequilibrium problem in the Soviet economy turned rapidly into one of macroeconomic instability, and what policy measures could be adopted in the Soviet context to deal with it. The Soviet leadership's decisions on the perestroika reform process did reflect this changing reality, both in some of the halting macroeconomic policy measures adopted and, more dramatically, in the postponement of price reforms.

With macroeconomic stability as the objective, the planners initiated measures aimed at reducing the budget deficit in 1989 and increasing the supplies of consumer goods via imports and accelerated domestic production. Defense capacities were to be pressed increasingly into producing consumer items. As for a monetary policy to control excessive wage payments by enterprises, it did not go beyond the announcement of an interest charge on enterprise borrowings. The measure was not enforced. The public was offered alternative assets, such as apartments, and consumer durables (for future delivery in exchange for a downpayment) with the aim of soaking up excessive liquidity. Currency reform, however, was ruled out completely.

Among the measures aimed at trimming the budget deficit were defense and investment cuts. Defense spending in 1989 and 1990 was planned to be cut by 14 percent, and military hardware by 19 percent. According to Central Intelligence Agency estimates (U.S. Congress, 1990, 11), Soviet defense spending declined in 1989 by 4 to 5 percent (in constant 1982 rubles) and weapons procurement by 6 to 7 percent.

Next, investment spending in the budget was scheduled to be cut by 7.5 billion rubles in 1989 and by at least 8 billion rubles in 1990 (*Izvestiia*, March 30, 1989)—the first such cuts in postwar Soviet history (U.S. Congress, 1989, 14). As a result of the actual cutback, investment spending went up by a miniscule 0.6 percent in 1989 (U.S. Congress, 1990, table C-5).

These cuts are unlikely to provide continuing relief to the budget deficit in 1990. The 1990 deficit may go up from 60 to 90 billion rubles because of lower profits from industry, 9 billion rubles in payment of higher procurement prices to grain farmers, pension increases, and new spending to relocate villagers from the areas contaminated by the Chernobyl nuclear accident (*Izvestiia*, June 15, 1990).

As for consumer goods, more were available from domestic production and imports but not enough to satisfy public demand at the fixed prices. The Central Intelligence Agency estimate (U.S. Congress, 1990, table C-3) of the growth of per capita consumption in constant 1982 prices in 1989 was 3 percent—most of it accounted for by a sharp rise in alcohol production and imports. The share of consumer goods imports in 1989, from razor blades to detergent, largely credit-financed, was planned to rise to 10 percent of the import bill. The switch to consumer goods production in defense factories was slow, however (ibid., 17).

In the meantime, in the absence of an effective monetary restraint, wage incomes were surging forward. As early as

March 1988 (*Izvestiia*, March 30, 1988), the finance minister had announced that loans for financing inventories would be subjected to a 15 percent interest charge. That policy, alas, was not implemented. Enterprises continued borrowing virtually cost-free and paying wages in excess of productivity gains. The Supreme Soviet therefore passed a law (*Izvestiia*, September 22, 1989) imposing a tax on excessive increase in wage funds. Consumer goods enterprises were exempted, however, from this penalty.

There was progress on the offer of alternative assets to the public with a view to soaking up the ruble overhang. But the results so far are disappointing. According to a special decree, residents of apartments could buy them by paying half their price, with the balance payable over ten years. In 1989, however, private occupants bought only 35,800 of the 76 million apartments in the country (*Pravda*, May 20, 1990). A recent presidential decree (ibid.) directing the Supreme Soviet to enact the necessary law carried the process further by allowing citizens to build, buy, and sell houses and own the land on which they stand. The process will undoubtedly take some years to gather speed.

This ragbag of measures failed to stabilize the consumer goods market. Thereafter, two packages followed in quick succession aimed at bringing the situation under control. The first was the Twelfth Five-Year Plan announced by Prime Minister Ryzhkov and adopted by the Congress of People's Deputies in December (*Pravda*, December 15, 1989). As a result, state orders for the production of essential items were imposed on consumer goods factories. The second package, also introduced by Ryzhkov in May 1990 (*Pravda*, May 25, 1990), announced price rises on a variety of items with a view to unfolding a "regulated market economy." They consisted of a tripling of bread prices as of July 1 and a doubling of some consumer goods prices (including meat) by January 1. Only 15 percent of the consumer goods items were to be subjected to the challenge of the market forces.*

* The weights of these items in consumer spending and in value-added are the important statistics in assessing the plan. But they are not clear.

These packages, following in quick succession, suggest that Gorbachev and his government are clearly searching for a workable transition to market-type arrangements. The optimal strategy of transiting to a system with price flexibility has so far eluded them and remains the top item on their agenda. An understanding of the general issues concerning the pace and sequencing of reforms during the transition is critical for making the transition. I discuss these broader issues and principles below and conclude with specific suggestions for the task facing the Soviet leader.

BIG BANG VERSUS THE ECONOMICS OF HASTENING SLOWLY

The criticism by the proponents of rapid price reform that "piecemeal" reforms have backfired, that Gorbachev has "wasted five years," that "one cannot cross a chasm in two leaps," is currently in vogue. It is by no means convincing.

Broad Principles

· Arguments by analogy can mislead. Single leaps across a chasm sound spectacular. But they require that Steven Spielberg is around to ensure that you get to the other side. Otherwise, you drop a bridge: admittedly a slower task. Gorbachev has arguably been doing that.

· Politically, he had to navigate around the conservatives, neutralizing Ligachev and his followers. Their absence from public view (until recently at the Twenty-eighth Party Congress) now should not induce amnesia about the arduous task that Gorbachev faced and accomplished. Their continuing presence, even though diminished relative to when Gorbachev became General Secretary five years ago, still requires agility to make reforms palatable, while occasionally infuriating the radical reformers, by linguistically masking their true content. Thus, the wide-ranging reform on "private property" (discussed earlier) did not use that phrase, any more than President Bush can let the word "taxes" be read on his lips even while he ponders "revenue enhancement" now.

But, politics aside, the notion that one must jump to total reform, with all the components of the ultimately desired economic system enacted into policy at once, is not sensible. Even for reform on a single dimension, such as the liberalization of trade via abolition of restrictions and duties, Adam Smith (whose doctrines drive the reforms) had the following sensible caveat to offer against freeing up trade in one fell swoop:

> It may sometimes be a matter of deliberation, how far, or in what manner it is proper to restore the free importation of foreign goods . . . when particular manufacturers, by means of high duties or prohibitions upon all foreign goods which can come into competition with them, have been so far extended as to employ a great multitude of hands. Humanity may in this case require that freedom of trade should be restored only by slow graduations, and with a good deal of reserve and circumspection. (Quoted in Irwin, 1989, 57)

Indeed, Sir Robert Peel, who repealed the English Corn Laws in 1846 to usher in free trade in the first dramatic economic reform somewhat comparable in importance to the Soviet task at hand, experimented with a milder relaxation of import duties at first, wanting to see how this worked. Later, when opting for total repeal, he cited Adam Smith's caution with approval, adding: "These are the words of the theoretical writer—of a writer not responsible for the practical application of his view, but they correspond with the doctrine of the practical reformer" (ibid.).

And then, Gorbachev's objective is far more complex than Adam Smith's: he must move away from an entire *system*, not just one policy (no matter how important) within it.

· Indeed, when the final objective or the desired "steady state" (in economic jargon) of a reformed economic system consists of several components, it is clear that there may be different political and economic roadblocks facing each one of them. Take the privatization component in the Soviet context. The political constraint on immediate reform arose from the conservative ideological forces at the outset, whereas the economic constraint continues to arise from the inevitable time lags in implementing the Property Law. Indeed, time has elapsed in locating buyers for apartments now for sale, and, as I observed earlier, the extent of privatization to date is miniscule.

· In short, given the different speeds at which even agreed-upon reform components can be pursued and implemented, piecemeal reform is inevitable. Metaphorical agendas of "big bangs" and "single leaps" obfuscate rather than clarify the analysis. The really important analytical questions, then, are:

1. Once the components of the desired economic reform have been identified, what are the political and economic constraints on each?

2. In light of the different speeds at which these components can be pursued, how is a transition path that must necessarily reflect these constraints to be devised such that it ensures a successful transition?

The latter question is the hardest to tackle since political judgments are involved at each stage. For instance, progress in one area, with inevitably slower progress in another, may create a temporary decline in income. But, if the government can ride out the temporary setback, it could later result in an increment in efficiency. This may happen also because the "imbalance" facilitates a creative policy response and speeds the pace at which the lagging sector can be reformed. For example, letting the cooperatives expand freely (without the meaningless financial restrictions currently under consideration) could create an exodus of skilled manpower from Soviet state enterprises, but this may prompt the policy makers to react creatively by rapidly leasing or privatizing the state units. Alternatively, the transition itself would be threatened if, reacting negatively to the initial deterioration from unbalanced progress, the populace too settles into a revolution of falling expectations from the reforming government, imperiling its legitimacy and its ability to stay the course.

· But if piecemeal reform is inevitable in the nature of the case,* the general notion that reform, when it is piecemeal, is necessarily bad, either immediately or in the long run or both, is simplistic and perhaps dangerous because of its superficial appeal. Consider the following example. A full move to currency convertibility is ultimately desirable, but it could be hazardous when confidence in the economy's strength and perestroika's success is low: it would lead to capital flight of a serious proportion, just as "human capital" has begun to emigrate recently because restrictions on emigration have been eased substantially. Hence, the prudent course again (remembering that even Ludwig Erhard, the great architect of postwar Germany's economic miracle and the celebrated pioneer of "big bangs," did not adopt even current-account convertibility at once) would be to proceed slowly by adopting innovations along the way, such as exchange auctions and "export retention" or "export bonus" schemes in which exporters are permitted to retain part of their hard-currency earnings for their own use. These intermediate devices will somehow bring trade and economic decisions closer to the "true" price of foreign exchange, moving the economy progressively to fuller reform.

Assessing Gorbachev's Policies in Light of Broad Principle

Keeping these conceptual clarifications and fresh perspectives in view, I now assess Gorbachev's attempts at reforming the Soviet economy during his five-year tenure to date, focusing on key issues rather than on detail.

---

* Even a "big bang" policy of simultaneous and instant policy announcements will necessarily encounter reality and the rate of effective *implementation* on different components of the package will diverge, yielding piecemeal reform.

· First, consider the question of price reform. It cannot be emphasized enough that Gorbachev stressed the need for price reform as early as June 1988 at the Party Conference. In doing so, Gorbachev, the confirmed socialist, sounded like a longtime bachelor advocating matrimony: "Everything rests now on the reform of the method of forming prices. I refer to the need for reviewing wholesale, retail, and state procurement prices. The fact that this issue remains unsettled unduly complicates the realization of economic reform. We cannot create normal economic relations in the economy or ensure correct valuations of expenditures and outputs and exchange of goods and services without reforming prices. Nor can we stimulate scientific-technical progress or efficient use of resources or normal markets" (*Pravda*, June 17, 1988).

His stand on the problem of the continuing budgetary subsidization of retail food items was equally forthright: "The situation is abnormal. Howsoever difficult the problem, whatever doubts and concerns it may raise initially, it is imperative that we resolve it" (ibid.). The context suggests that the need for removing subsidies was prompted more by the microeconomic efficiency view that subsidies "distort" prices than by the implication that subsidies added to macroeconomic disequilibrium.

· Even as Gorbachev was emphasizing the urgency of reforming prices and removing subsidies, the underlying situation, as I have argued above, was changing for the worse. The budget deficit was increasing sharply, consumer goods production was lagging relative to investment goods output, and wages were running ahead of productivity. There was too much cash, not enough consumer goods, and Gorbachev was talking about changing prices and removing subsidies! The public reacted by writing angry letters expressing doubts about the intentions of the leadership and accusing it of ignoring the welfare of the people. Just as goods started disappearing from state stores, rationing appeared in a number of cities (*Sotsialisticheskaia industriia*, November 18, 1988).

Gorbachev's response was predictable too. Nine months later, at a Central Committee meeting in mid-March 1989, he declared a changed position: "Prices should not be tampered with at present. Consumer demand for goods and food items is not yet satisfied. We have not yet begun the critical steps for stabilizing the finances of the economy. We need two to three years to restore the health of the economy, stabilize the finances and the markets." The signal from Gorbachev was thus for a two-stage reform strategy: first, stabilize the economy, as it were, getting the macroeconomic situation under control; then move to price reform. The microeconomic reform must be built on macroeconomic stabilization.

Thus, price reform would follow at the end of the first stage (lasting two to three years) during which the budget deficit would be trimmed and consumer goods supplies would improve. On several occasions the Ryzhkov-Abalkin team also emphasized the prior need to set up the infrastructure for a functioning market (among them property, banking, and tax reform legislation) and guaranteeing welfare benefits to vulnerable groups (Rumer, 1990). Thus, the leadership's thinking represented a two-stage process that would unfold at deliberate speed, short of a "big bang." The first stage of macrostabilization and infrastructural legislation must precede the next stage of price reform.

The Twelfth Five-Year Plan announced by Prime Minister Ryzhkov and approved by the Supreme Soviet in December 1989 (*Pravda*, December 15, 1989) incorporated this two-stage reform strategy. It included the earlier scheme formulated by Deputy Prime Minister Leonid Abalkin (*Izvestiia*, October 24, 1989; *Pravda*, November 14, 1989) and did not mark a departure from Abalkin's formulation. In fact, the Abalkin document was appended to the Ryzhkov plan. Abalkin, too, had argued that, in the first stage of the plan's implementation, the budget deficit should be reduced by cutting centrally financed investments (largely in heavy industry), thereby tilting resource allocation in the economy toward consumer goods. Furthermore, as announced by Ryzhkov, the increased supply of *essential* consumer goods in 1990 and beyond was to be ensured via state orders in consumer goods industries. This step was intended to prevent consumer goods factories from diverting capacities to the production of higher-priced, fancy items with a lucrative market.

As a transitional, crisis-management measure, the Ryzhkov Plan could be argued to have a defensible rationale. Soviet enterprises do deliver when they are required to fulfill targets on a priority basis—this time, essential consumer goods. At the same time, the infrastructure for a successful price reform, such as the private ownership of assets, lifetime lease of land, and banking and tax reforms, was not yet enacted. Price reform would be ill-advised without laying the legal foundations for creating the necessary institutions and policies for incentives to operate.

· But no sooner was the ink dry than the plan was overtaken by two new forces, one economic and the other political. By official count (*Izvestiia*, April 7, 1990), the growth of the economy continued its slide, showing a negative growth rate in the first quarter of 1990 (over the first quarter of 1989). Consumer goods output grew by 6.4 percent, but industrial output declined by 1.2 percent, and average monthly earnings ballooned by 9 percent. Ryzhkov had slapped back the output targets on consumer goods enterprises but had overlooked the imperative of enforcing wage and monetary restraint.

Shortages continued to intensify in early 1990. In the atmosphere of panic, very few were interested in rational explanations. The decline in the industrial production index led to hyped-up accounts of vastly greater declines in GNP, current and prospective. There was little allowance for the fact that the transformation of heavy industry and defense capacities to the production of consumer goods could cause both transitional decline in output and misleading decline in the overall output index because different goods had different weights. Such benign explanations lost out to the malign ones attributing the decline to "growing chaos" and "piecemeal reform." In circulating exaggerated accounts of the economy's decline, some economists in the Soviet Union and abroad contributed to the feeling that apocalypse was around the corner. Some suggested that since the shortages signified collapsing production—why bother sorting out the alternative causes of shortages, including distribution problems?—no time should be lost in jettisoning the old system and embracing full price flexibility. It was up to Gorbachev and his advisers to work out a package, implement it, and take the consequences. The plan must go so that the market could march in. Others surmised that, given the potential for hyperinflation, the option of letting prices go all at once would require tough wage and monetary discipline for checking the inflationary spiral: if massive unemployment followed, so be it. That was Poland's way, the road of "shock therapy." That too, in this view, was Gorbachev's headache. Of course, as the leader in charge of implementing reforms, Gorbachev followed his instincts and turned down the shock therapy.

Alarming as the accounts of economic performance were, even more worrisome were the results of the winter 1990 elections which brought radical reformers to power in a few cities and increased their presence in republic legislatures. The voters, it seemed, wanted a reform momentum. In the meantime, however, Gorbachev was elected President with wide powers, and the critical legislation on abolishing the monopoly of the Communist Party, the Property Law, and the Land Legislation had been passed. The remaining laws on banking and tax reform, setting up the financial infrastructure, were to follow soon. The time was ripe for a decisive move: the political pressures from the increasingly vocal reformers, Gorbachev's consolidation of his Presidential position, and completion of the bulk of his legislative agenda implied that he was finally ready to bite the bullet.

· Against this background, the next Ryzhkov-Abalkin plan of May 22, 1990, announcing a threefold increase in the price of bread by July 1 and a twofold increase in some

Fɪɢ. 10.4. Gorbachev is fearful of being gobbled up by the sick bear if he proceeds forthwith to cure it with strong economic medicine. Reprinted from *The Washington Post*, National Weekly Edition, June 4–10, 1990. (Copyright 1990 Buffalo News. Reprinted with permission of Universal Press Syndicate. All rights reserved.)

consumer items by January 1, 1991, and introducing flexible prices in 15 percent of consumer goods marked a denouement. Concerned about the effects of these price increases on standards of living of "vulnerable" groups such as the pensioners, the planners included indexed compensation, thus building in inflationary pressures rather than scotching them.

This plan admits partial price flexibility and builds in price increases that could, on balance, save on subsidies that currently strain the budget. It is, however, too timid, proceeds too slowly toward price reform, and leaves open the possibility that fuller price flexibility may not be the ultimate objective.

· The situation now calls out for fuller price reform from several directions. To repeat, the legislation for such reform is finally in place. Policies, such as leasing and privatization, are being pursued. The conservatives are no longer the dire threat they were when Gorbachev came on stage. The growth of partial reforms has also created pressures on the system (as I discussed earlier) for further reforms. Recall the new ability of farms to bypass implicit taxation in state purchases leading to offers of higher procurement prices on grain in early May 1990 and, in turn, pushing the government also to charge higher prices for bread—all this inadvertently bringing the whole situation closer to a market regimen than before; recall again how the enhanced freedom of enterprises to import results in excess import demands that (while met by trade credits, gold sales, and running down of reserves) push the system, ever so slowly, to incentive-oriented schemes such as exchange auctions.

In short, the time has finally come for Gorbachev's team to take the bolder, faster steps to markets and price flexibility. The claim that he "wasted five years" evidently does not survive careful scrutiny. But he should now be ready to change gears and move into the next stage of the two-stage process. I conclude, therefore, with a brief analysis of what the strategy in this next lap of an arduous race must be.

PERESTROIKA: WHAT NOW?

A coherent plan that controls the macroeconomic situation with the policy tools now at hand and fulfills the microeconomic objectives of price reform is now feasible and necessary. Its components can be spelled out as follows.

· On the macroeconomic front, the privatization process must continue, creating the assets that can be an alternative to cash holdings. But this is an inevitably slow process and increasingly seen to be so everywhere, even in fast-moving Poland. Evidently, a currency reform such as a partial freeze of the personal holdings of bank balances (discussed above), for say three to five years, would do the necessary job of preventing an inflationary price spiral as prices are freed. As incomes and investments grow with the price reform, and stabilization takes root, the "desired" money balances will rise to match the frozen balances, which can then be released without serious inflationary consequences. New assets will also have become available through ongoing privatization. The planners ought to view this as a less painful, and more efficient, option to pursue than the cruder method of relying excessively on the monetary brakes to resolve the macroeconomic dilemma with resulting unemployment and recession.

· A wage or incomes policy is absolutely essential for maintaining the microeconomic discipline. The example of Poland, with rising unemployment, demonstrates the results of applying sharp monetary brakes. Indeed, the absence of wage discipline will perforce require a heavy dose of monetary restraint to control the resulting inflation, with severe unemployment as its consequence. A social contract on wages is absolutely essential during the transition to a market system if not beyond. Gorbachev will have to pull together the diversifying political leadership and groups in persuading the unions to accept the necessary discipline as a way of *avoiding* serious (macro) unemployment during the transition. The miners and railway workers need to be reminded that there is a trade-off between wage restraint and unemployment as tools of macroeconomic policy in the market system to which a transition is desired, and that the former is the preferred alternative. But as prices change and rise, the planners will need to work up a different policy tool, which I suggest below, to deal with the problem of income distribution.

· While the macroeconomic dimensions of the required policy are relatively well understood, the question of price flexibility in its microeconomic aspects is not. Contrary to the general view that all prices be let loose forthwith, there are two main exceptions that must be made.

1. Economists distinguish between "natural" and artificial monopolies. Some industries are natural monopolies

in the sense that economies of scale require large operations relative to the size of the market. There is no competition because the market can accommodate only one or a few firms. Potential rivals do not get into the industry because they find such entry neither possible nor profitable. On the other hand, a monopoly may be created by artificial barriers to the entry of rival firms, as when the authorities prevent new firms from getting into the industry and even eliminate competition from foreign firms by restricting imports.

With artificial monopolies, the solution is relatively straightforward if the political will is there: the barriers can be lifted. But with natural monopolies, economists have a harder time. They advocate instead the regulation of prices in the social interest.

As it happens, in Soviet industry, there are currently many de facto natural monopolies, reflecting gigantomania and the preference for vertical integration. For example, machine building in the capitalist West is scattered, and manufacturers buy rolled steel from outside. By contrast, in a giant Soviet machine-building plant, iron ore goes in at one end and machines come out at the other in a sequence of integrated operations. There is no scope here for subcontracting. At the same time, central planners through the years have located large plants in areas of their choice. The result is often, as with the single factory in Lithuania supplying ice-cream cones over a vast area, the creation of monopolies. Large plants were created that cannot be subdivided by governmental policies aimed at breaking up monopolies. In machine building alone, more than two-thirds of the items are produced by one or two enterprises (*Ekonomika i zhizn'* 13, March 1990, 5).

As a result, while the problem will ease over time as more factories are built and new entrants get in, for the present the many indestructible Soviet monopolies will have to be subjected to price regulation—the no-no word for some. At the same time, the monopolies should be freed from ministerial control over their production and investment decisions. Abolishing the ministries rather than abolishing the monopolies should be the first order of the day.

2. But if the above monopoly-based argument for regulated prices applies to heavy industry, in the main, there is an altogether different rationale against freeing all consumer goods prices. Gorbachev is rightly worried that price reform would raise prices of important consumer goods and create popular unrest. As a result, the Ryzhkov-Abalkin plan of May 22, 1990, included indexing to protect "vulnerable" groups and limited price flexibility to only a small group of items. His economic adviser, Nikolai Petrakov (*New York Times*, June 10, 1990), has subsequently criticized the indexing solution as potentially inflationary and proposed instead that, while most prices should be freed, the prices of basic essentials—for example, meat with fat—should be controlled to ensure living standards. But the problem is that, if you fix the prices of essentials while letting other prices rise, the iron law of markets tells you that the supply of essentials dries up! For example, housing shortage is the inexorable consequence of rent control. The supply of housing can be restored only if the government steps in with a housing program, "shifting the supply curve to the right." But the whole point of the Soviet reform is to take the government out of the market, and Petrakov's plan does not disagree with that objective.

A sensible and feasible solution to the income-distributional worry that combines fixed and flexible pricing in a coherent framework is to be found instead in the "dual pricing" system successfully practiced in countries of South Asia (especially India). Following it, a minimal basket of consumption items such as meat, bread, sugar, and cooking oil (mentioned by Prime Minister Ryzhkov in a recent interview) would be made available, in fixed rations per individual, at fixed prices in state stores. But, beyond that, everything would be bought and sold in unregulated, free markets everywhere. Thus, the system would combine elements of guaranteed access of a minimum basket to everyone in state stores, while letting the market incentives operate freely for the rest. The implied subsidy for the guaranteed distribution through state "fair price shops" can be financed, partly or fully, by explicit agricultural taxation. The tax revenue can be used to purchase the basket of essential items in the market for subsequent distribution at lower prices in state stores.*

The Soviet planners can readily adopt the dual-pricing system. The shops are already state-owned and distribute items coming through the state supply system. It should be easy to convert some of them into fair price shops where specific quantities can be bought by citizens who would have been issued "ration" cards for the purpose. Such an arrangement could also involve local soviets and, as it happens, the radical reformers (now in charge of a few cities) in the chores of implementing the scheme. The current ad hoc system with unseemly sights of citizens scrambling for whatever sausage they can lay their hands on needs to be replaced by a formal arrangement guaranteeing a minimum amount to everyone. Beyond that and for the rest of the consumer goods, they will face free markets and fuller shelves in other shops.

Finally, a suggestion on joint ventures. An important lesson for the Soviet planners to consider is that most developing countries, including some on the margin of subsistence, have allowed limited convertibility of their currencies for repatriation of profits by foreigners. The Soviet Union surely can follow suit by qualifying the right to repatriate by imposing a grace period before such repatriation begins and rapidly approving foreign ventures that offer enforceable guarantees to promote exports from the Soviet Union. The continuing foreign exchange burden which such a qualified repatriation will impose on the So-

---

* The flexible-price market provides the necessary incentive to produce more. The exact impact on supply, under the dual-pricing system, relative to the impact when there is a single flexible price, depends on several factors, but economic analysis shows that it need not be less favorable. At the same time, the guarantee of minimum supplies of essentials at fixed prices should help moderate the opposition that erupted on June 14, 1990, when the Soviet legislators turned down the tripling of bread prices proposed on May 22.

viet Union can be eased by medium and long-term credits from the West. Such credits will facilitate a speedy entry by Western private enterprise in Soviet industry and infrastructure.*

A coherent plan that weaves these policy elements together should make Gorbachev's task that much easier. But ultimately, getting a package accepted in the Supreme Soviet and by the public at large is a formidable political task. A "social contract" of the Polish variety giving him a popular mandate is beyond Gorbachev's grasp at present. It is doubtful if any Soviet politician, Yeltsin included, can manage that. But is it possible that the Soviet leader, in an arrangement similar to the French "cohabitation model," will discard his present team of cabinet members and economic planners and form a multiparty government with significant representation of the reformers? Some of the reformers in the Interregional Group in the Congress of People's Deputies, among them Sergei Stankevich (deputy mayor of Moscow) and Anatoly Sobchak (mayor of Leningrad), may opt for Gorbachev if he were finally to recognize popular pressures, renounce "reform communism," and kick the ladder. Will he do that?

Some doubt that he can (Sestanovich, 1990). But the Soviet leader has, time and again, discarded old positions in a show of decisive pragmatism while choosing his own moment and manner to adopt new ones. Within a year of having declared that a multiparty system was "rubbish," he led the fight in the Central Committee in early February 1990 for the abolition of Article 6 of the Soviet Constitution granting the monopoly of power to the Communist Party.

* At the July Houston summit of the Western industrial countries, West Germany and France were solidly in favor of advancing credits to the Soviet Union whereas President Bush offered technical assistance without cash to rebuild Soviet infrastructure, including rail and communications networks, grain silos, and food distribution systems. Such a specific package was designed to placate the domestic conservative lobby, which argued that the Soviet Union continued to shy away from decisive market reforms, to spend vast amounts on defense, and to assist Cuba. Targeting U.S. assistance to specific programs, in this view, would promote market reforms and prevent its diversion to defense and to Cuba.

Rejecting his initial commitment to state ownership of means of production, he steered in spring 1990 the adoption by the Supreme Soviet of the Property Law and the Land Legislation. At the Washington summit, he was ready to be seen in the company of the top brass of American capitalism suggesting that they bring investments and technology to the Soviet Union. Currently, the lesson of the Yeltsin election to the presidency of the Russian Republic, and of his stunning resignation from the Communist Party at the Party Congress, could not have been lost on Gorbachev, namely, that the threat to perestroika's stability arises more from the radical reformers than from the conservatives.

Even with a coalition government in place, Gorbachev himself may cease being President if, reacting to a refurbished economic package, the coal miners and the railway workers go on strike and literally bring the country to a halt. He can be removed from the presidency by a vote in the Congress of People's Deputies. That is a chance he must take. It is unlikely, however, that he will then wilt in quiet retirement. He may still stage a comeback in a future election and be the leader of the opposition. While the economic largesse of perestroika will be long in coming, the political rewards of glasnost' are already at hand. The nature of Soviet politics has really changed, perhaps beyond Gorbachev's own calculations. But that will remain his permanent contribution, irrespective of what the future has in store for his countrymen in these turbulent times.

When Prime Minister Nehru of India was asked what he would like to be remembered for, he was reported to have singled out his contribution to nurturing the potential of "400 million Indians to govern themselves." In an informal conversation with members of the Young Communist League (*Pravda*, April 12, 1990), a youngster asked Gorbachev if he had a successor in mind. Gorbachev replied: "I do not but perhaps he is present in this room." What more valuable legacy can a Soviet politician leave behind?

Illustrating the Economic Reform and Its Inadequacy

In the text, I have discussed the inadequacies of the economic reform in regard to its conception of how markets function (chapter 5). In consequence, it offers an extremely limited type of reform.

To show this more clearly, I offer here a stylized illustrative analysis, drawing on the familiar general-equilibrium tools. I first deal with static efficiency, then with dynamic efficiency.

STATIC EFFICIENCY

In figure A.1, let AB be the production possibility frontier; for a linear utility function, P^* is then the efficient production point. It corresponds to P^* in the underlying box diagram of figure A.2 with the given endowments $\bar{K}$ and $\bar{L}$ of the two productive factors and the production functions for the two goods, X and Y.

1. When factors of production are allocated by central planners, rather than by efficient factor markets, production is off the efficient contract curve in figure A.2, at $\hat{P}$. The corresponding production is shown at $\hat{P}$ inside the production possibility curve in figure A.1. In terms of Hicksian equivalent-variational measures, the loss from such allocative inefficiency is ST in figure A.1. This is the loss actually measured for Soviet industry in Desai and Martin (1983) and Thornton (1971).

2. But there is an added element of loss, RS, since production further shifts inside from $\hat{P}$ to $\hat{\hat{P}}$ in the Soviet economic reality faced by Gorbachev. The overwhelming state ownership of enterprises, combined with the inefficiency-prone criteria under which they have functioned, doubly reduces technical productivity below what is built into the "maximal" isoquants in figure A.2. For example, state ownership, combined with the dominance of a single party and its apparatus of surveillance and intrusion into the economic sector, accentuates in no small measure the problems of X-inefficiency that continue plaguing pub-

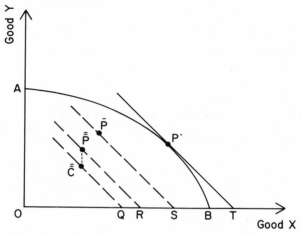

FIG. A.1. Static Efficiency: ST = loss due to alloca-
tional inefficiency resulting from nonfunctioning
capital and labor markets; RS = loss from X-ineffi-
ciency and DUP activities; QR = loss from mismatching of supplies and demands resulting in continuing
disequilibrium.

lic-sector enterprises even in mixed economies and pluralistic
regimes. These consist of loafing, lack of attention to costs, overstaffing, and poor organization of the work force on the factory
floor, among others. Indeed, these problems have fueled recent
drives in the Third World toward privatization as a possible
cure.[11]

In addition, one can include here the losses that arise from
what Kornai (1980) calls "soft budget" constraints and Western
literature calls Directly Unproductive Profit-seeking (DUP) activities (Bhagwati 1982). Here, resources such as managerial time, for
example, are spent to get around an endless maze of political and
economic restrictions on economic activity, thus diverting these
resources from productive to unproductive activity.[12] There is
also the loss of time spent by a typical Soviet manager in filling
out forms to be sent to higher authorities. The general manager
of a machine-building plant was speaking from experience when
he said at the June Party Conference: "It is useless to fight the
forms. You have got to kill the people who produce them"
(*Pravda*, July 1, 1988).

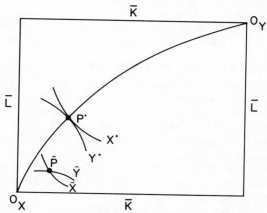

FIG. A.2. Static Efficiency. Resource-allocational inefficiency takes the Soviet economy off the contract curve from P^* to $\hat{P}$ where resources are still fully employed.

3. Finally, the story goes even beyond $\hat{\hat{P}}$ since the Soviet system, as discussed in the text, notoriously fails to match supplies and demands—far more so than capitalist systems. Typically, and persistently, therefore, there are shortages and surpluses. Thus, while production occurs at $\hat{\hat{P}}$, the situation illustrated in figure A.1 is one in which consumption takes place at $\hat{\hat{C}}$: $\hat{\hat{C}}\hat{\hat{P}}$ is the persistent surplus of unwanted or unutilizable good Y whereas, at the given income, there is excess demand for good X. Thus, a further loss of QR is imposed by this "ill-fitting, jigsaw-puzzle" effect.

ECONOMIC REFORM AND STATIC EFFICIENCY

Therefore, it is obvious that the economic reform, as currently planned, offers only limited forays into each of these elements of static inefficiency.

Allocative Efficiency Effect (ST)

The cooperative sector can be thought of as introducing an element of factor mobility since cooperatives can enter and exit without severe restrictions. But they are essentially limited to light manufacturing and services. The question of factor mobility in the very large and dominant state sector is still an open one, though here, there is discussion now of encouraging labor mobility. The actual plans in this respect are, however, limited.

X-Efficiency, DUP Activities, and Other Aspects (RS)

Some gains are likely from the improvement of X-efficiency. These will arise from greater incentives and initiatives for managers and workers. The size of the gains will depend on whether ministerial intrusion is minimized. For example, DUP-type losses will persist if enterprise labor collectives must continue spending resources in fighting the "petty tutelage" of ministries by taking recourse to the legal guarantees provided under the Law. The recent case (*Izvestiia*, March 23, 1988) of the giant machine-building works, Uralmash, illustrates such losses pointedly. The worker collective protested that the items for which state orders were assigned by the Ministry of Heavy and Transport Machinery were not in demand and were unprofitable. The orders were rescinded after a court action but were, typically, transferred to another machine-building unit.

Ill-fitting Jigsaw-Puzzle Effect (QR)

The introduction of the "demand-determined" contract system should go some way toward eliminating the mismatch of supplies and demands, *given* the (im)mobility of capital and labor across enterprises. However, the beneficial effect will be small as long as capacities cannot be expanded and contracted. It will be limited to mismatches arising from lack of information, which can be remedied if buyers materialize for what is produced.

ECONOMIC REFORM AND DYNAMIC EFFICIENCY

While the preceding analysis focuses on components of static efficiency, markets in capitalist economies operate so as to permit, and even prompt, entrepreneurs to take risks, produce in anticipation of demand, innovate with new products, and generally to act as Schumpeterian entrepreneurs rather than rentiers. These are the mainsprings of capitalist growth. There will be very little of this in the current economic reform.

Figure A.3 illustrates this dynamic aspect. Whereas figure A.1 showed the Soviet economy operating well *inside* a one-time production possibility curve owing to several successive sources of

FIG. A.3. Dynamic Efficiency. With inadequate introduction of market, economic reform offers very limited dynamic efficiency advantages, implying shift of P^* to P^{**} whereas substantive market reform, as discussed in the text, would lead more productively to P^{***}.

static inefficiency, figure A.3 shows the consequences of the failure to address markets meaningfully. It will confine the Soviet economy to small dynamic gains—shifting the production possibility frontier outward from P^* to P^{**}—whereas substantive reforms would have promised a more significant yield (shifting production out from P^* to P^{***}).[13]

Political Structure and Election Procedures

The Soviet Union consists of fifteen Union Republics. The largest, the Russian Republic (RSFSR), spans the breadth of the land over eleven time zones. There are thirty-eight autonomous units within the republics. For example, Nagorno-Karabakh, frequently in the news because of clashes there between Armenians and Azerbaijanis, is an Autonomous Region (*oblast*), with a majority of Armenians, in the Union Republic of Azerbaijan.

The cardinal features of the political arrangement throughout the territorial hierarchy, from the Union to the village, are a party organization and a governmental organization. Your guess is right: the former dominates the latter.

THE PARTY

The supreme body at the top of the current party hierarchy is the Congress. It meets every five years, makes important policy announcements, lays down major guidelines, and elects the Central Committee. The Central Committee, with over three hundred members, is the policy-making body on a day-to-day basis. It is helped in its chores by the party Secretariat, which contains various departments. Mikhail Gorbachev was once in charge of agriculture in the Secretariat. (In a sweeping change on September 30, 1988, the departments were abolished and replaced by six commissions.) The actual direction and control of policies is in the hands of the inner sanctum—the Politburo.

This party organization is repeated on a territorial basis at all levels except the lowest. Thus, except for the Russian Republic (RSFSR), the republics have their five-year party congresses, committees, secretariats, and buros. By contrast, the Russian Republic contributes a large fraction of the membership of the all-Union bodies. The party structure is repeated down the territorial line in regions, cities and towns, and urban and rural districts.

The primary (i.e., the lowest-level) party units are at the work place—in the factories and farms, in educational institutions, in the army and the KGB, and in offices. Their composition depends on the size of the establishment, but three Communists or more can form a party unit. One becomes the secretary, the second the deputy secretary, and the third constitutes the membership. A party committee is generally formed in establishments with more than three hundred members. The smaller ones manage with a buro.

Article 6 of the 1977 Soviet Constitution describes these party units as "the leading and guiding force of Soviet society and the nucleus of its political system." Members are expected to spread Marxist-Leninist teachings, advance the cause of "communist construction," and emphasize the vanguard role of the party inside the establishment and outside. But propaganda and persuasion have ultimately a limited appeal; so party control is enforced via more effective methods. The top personnel of an establishment are invariably included in the party unit and, in order to reach the top, one usually has to be a loyal Communist. One becomes a chief accountant, the story goes, when one knows not that "two plus two adds up to four" but that "two plus two adds up to what the party boss wants it to be." As a matter of fact, party discipline is enforced by maintaining a list (*nomenklatura*) of critical appointments and dependable appointees.

THE GOVERNMENT

As with the party, the governmental organization is laid out in meticulous detail. The legislatures (soviets) and executive bodies (councils of ministers) are again organized on territorial lines. Below the republics, there are executive committees rather than councils of ministers, and the soviets are essentially administrative rather than legislative bodies.

At the apex is the Supreme Soviet, consisting of two houses with a membership of 750 each. It meets twice a year and gives legal stamp to the policies already decided by the party. The resolutions are adopted unanimously with a show of hands. Within the Supreme Soviet, specific functions are assigned to its Presidium, consisting of a president and several vice-presidents. The Presidium calls for elections and convenes Supreme Soviet sessions. It interprets laws, and ratifies and abrogates international treaties. It appoints and dismisses the military command, and can declare martial law and mobilize the armed forces if necessary. The list of its powers is impressive. But in reality the Presidium is a paper tiger: it cannot confront and override the wishes of the party on any important issue.

Down the line, the Union republics have their soviets and councils of ministers. Autonomous units, regions, cities and towns, urban and rural districts, and villages follow, with their soviets numbering over fifty thousand. They have their executive committees (which are elected at the first session of the soviets), and their administrative departments and permanent commissions. The soviets meet four or six times a year, and the executive committee, assisted by appropriate administrative departments manages its area of administration. The executive committee of the Moscow city soviet manages the city's hospitals, parks, transport services, housing, and the rest. Then there are members of the permanent commissions who supervise these activities.

What is the relationship between the soviet and the party committee at the various levels? The historical origin of the soviets is instructive in this regard. They were workers' committees with a proletarian backbone: they spearheaded the Revolution of 1917. Indeed, in the brief interval between the February and October revolutions, the Petrograd (Leningrad) soviet was active in toppling the Provisional Government. Later, soviets sprouted all over, and the Congress of Soviets wielded supreme authority. The word *soviet* (council) was made part of the country's name when the Soviet Union was formed in 1922. During the Stalin years, the soviets lost not only their revolutionary fervor but also their political power. True, the decisions of the party committee must be formally approved by the relevant soviet before they can be legal. This is especially so with regard to legislation that is initiated, debated, and drafted by the Central Committee and then formally approved by the Supreme Soviet. But there is no denying that, by now, the soviets have been reduced merely to approving the decisions of the party committees.

Gorbachev wants to revitalize the soviets. It is doubtful if he wants to follow Lenin, who, on the eve of the Bolshevik Revolution, adopted the slogan: "All power to the soviets." But he clearly intends the soviets to be sufficiently energized to fight interference from party committees in administration and management.

ELECTION PROCEDURES

The soviets must consist of independent members rather than party yes-men if these groups are to counter the pressures of party functionaries. Over the years, the name of only one candidate, approved by the party, has been placed on the ballot next to each position to be filled. The only way voters can register disapproval is by crossing out the candidate's name before casting the ballot. In the end, a candidate who is nominated gets elected; the only requirement is that he or she get a simple majority of the votes cast.

Nevertheless, all the frills of elections mark the process. Elections to the Supreme Soviet and the republic soviets take place every five years; those to the local soviets occur more frequently, every two and a half years. Candidates are put up by factory and farm collectives and other employees. There are voters' meetings where their merits are debated. Of course, the candidates must meet party guidelines, and the district party officials must make sure that the various groups of professionals, factory workers and farmers, and women are adequately represented. The candidates register themselves with the election commissions and are formally approved at voters' meetings. There is a three-week election campaign that includes election rallies, canvassing, and active discussion of various issues (local and national). Election is usually on a Sunday and voter turnout is large, exceeding 70 percent excluding absentee and proxy voters. All adults over the age of eighteen are qualified to vote. The parallels with pluralistic democracy are, however, superficial; the party dominates the choice of the candidates put on the slate for approval.

How to dilute this control of the party is the issue in reforming election procedures. In the post-Stalin years, there has been a continuing effort to pick a broad slate of candidates that would adequately represent the diverse interests of Soviet society. But party control in the choice has persisted. Gorbachev is not ready yet to promote genuine representation at the cost of party control. His objective to date is more realistic and limited—that is, retire the die-hard, anti-perestroika elements both from the party and the soviets at various levels. The first step would be to reform the procedures for electing the members of the party committees and the soviets. The proposed changes (which I discussed in chapter 6) relating to multiple candidates, the secret ballot, and limits on the tenure of office are to apply to both groups.

In one regard Gorbachev is following in the footsteps of Khrushchev, although with better preparation and greater success so far. At the Twenty-second Party Congress in 1961, several provisions were set out in Article 35 of the party rules prohibiting party committee members at various levels from being reelected, much as Gorbachev has managed to do at the June Party Conference. But Khrushchev's success was short-lived; the reform was rescinded at the next Congress.

Notes

1. Among recent contributions analyzing the economic reforms are Bergson (1987), Joint Economic Committee (JEC) (1987), Schroeder (1987), and Hewett (1988b).

2. Nor do the planners propose that a full-fledged capitalist market environment will eventually be created. True, Abel Aganbegyan (1988, 113) promises "competitive tendering" among enterprises for state orders; wholesale trade in materials will eventually replace state allocations (119); wholesale trade is envisaged also in the "means of production" (128); and "by the year 1990 no less than 60% of all production in the country is to be allocated through wholesale trading and by 1992 this share will rise to 80–90%" (137). "Centralized pricing will be retained only for the most essential products, to control their rate of growth and stave off inflation" (128).

At the same time, free movement of resources in response to market signals in a Schumpeterian setting is ruled out. "Land and natural resources cannot be bought and sold. Since there is no unemployment and the economic base of society accords with socialist ownership, there is no labour market. A market for capital is not envisaged as part of perestroika. There are no plans for a Soviet stock exchange, shares, bills of exchange or profit from commercial credit" (Aganbegyan 1988, 127). Accordingly, the renovation of the capital stock, as well as its pace, is to proceed under planned directives: "One third of current resources in the total volume of capital investment is spent on reconstruction. In the 1986–90 period this share is to be increased to at least a half. The volume of new construction should fall and it will be undertaken only when all possibilities available for increasing production from existing investment are exhausted. After due consideration, certain projects will be rapidly developed whereas others will be stopped totally or temporarily halted. A general inventory of capital goods is to be undertaken and programs are to be worked out for future technical reconstruction of every branch and every enterprise. The proportion of capital stock that will be rejected as obsolete, especially from the more active section of the economy, is to double in a short time. This will mean the renewal of more than one third of the productive plant with up to 50% new machinery by the end of 1990" (102–3).

Thus, the Soviet capital stock is to be renewed not on the basis of rational criteria of rates of return but, as before, under planners' directives.

3. In its market economy version, the static notion of economic efficiency implies that with unchanging demand and prices, a machine that saves materials or fuel is worth installing. The cost curve moves down and profits go up. However, in a dynamic setting, the demand for the items produced by the machine will have to be forecast accurately before the decision to install the machine is made.

This is not the notion of economic efficiency Aganbegyan has in mind. He writes: "From an economic point of view technological renewal can be considered as progress only when it assures a rise in economic efficiency. . . . If by renewal the economy is rid of one type of waste, for example the reduction of labour inputs, but simultaneously creates additional and still greater labour costs involved in increasing the capital stock, then this would not be progress but regress. Thus the economic evaluation of new technology must in our view be undertaken quite rigorously" (1988, 86).

Implicit here is the notion that productivity of the new machine or process should keep ahead of costs. That is the way it should be. But unless demand considerations are brought into the argument, this view of economic efficiency retains a production or "supply-side" orientation.

4. I have separated here the reforms in politics from other noneconomic reforms as a convenient device for analyzing the sequencing of Gorbachev's reforms.

5. Eventually, the removal of subsidies should help to contain inflation; in the short run, however, it results in higher prices that cut into real wages.

6. The insider-outsider dichotomy is relevant in this context: unions tend to maximize benefits to those who are inside (i.e., members) rather than the entire working class. This is also the problem with Martin Weitzman's (1986) innovative proposal for a share economy. Its adoption will generally imply lowering the average wage within a firm, thereby hurting the insiders. However, it is likely to benefit labor as a whole because it will ensure higher employment than existing methods of capitalist remuneration.

7. As I have noted, private industry that has functioned in a sheltered environment is not quite ready to welcome free markets in the developing countries.

8. Accordingly, in Appendix 1, where economic reforms are illustrated, I have assumed fixed prices.

9. It is not clear if these gains will materialize beyond 1990 as a result of the price reform. Aganbegyan (1988, 135) says that prices will be set by the planners only "for the more essential staple products." But will the remaining prices result from freely functioning markets? I am doubtful. For Aganbegyan states: "At the same time the sphere of contractually set and free prices will rapidly expand, since now enterprises themselves will decide on their own development plans based in turn on agreements with consumers. Thus to a large extent prices will be a matter of agreement. It is possible then that the state will set up a certain method for calculating prices, and the Price Committee is being invested with the task of assessing the rationale for contractual and free prices. In particular, speculative price increases aimed at excessive profit will not be permitted. Special measures will be taken to combat monopolies. It can be seen that a process of democratising the whole of price formation is underway" (1988, 135).

I have already noted that the prices mutually agreed upon by state-owned enterprises are subject to ceilings and therefore cannot be regarded as prices resulting from a free play of market forces. Also, the effective way to deal with "excessive profit" and to "combat monopolies" is to facilitate a free flow of resources in the desired directions rather than enforce price controls that will not work anyway.

10. However, it is true that this awareness, which has materialized gradually, is not reflected in the overly optimistic targets of the current Five-Year Plan (1986–1990), which was launched with Gorbachev's blessings.

11. See also my discussion of X-efficiency in the Soviet economy in Desai (1987, chap. 1).

12. Ibid.

13. In Figure A.3, I have omitted from consideration the static-inefficiency losses depicted in figure A.1 so as to concentrate attention on the dynamic-efficiency argument. Also, it should be noted that the production-possibility frontier will expand, even without economic reform, owing to accumulation of capital and labor and due to "normal" technical change.

References

Aganbegyan, Abel. 1988. *The Economic Challenge of Perestroika.* Bloomington: Indiana University Press.

Aslund, Anders. 1990a. "The Soviet Economy: From Bad to Worst." *The Washington Post,* National Weekly Edition. February 5–11.

———. 1990b. "Soviet Foreign Trade: Red Ink Rising." *The New York Times, Week in Review.* June 3.

Bergson, Abram. 1987. "The Gorbachev Revolution." *Challenge* 30 (September–October): 26–33.

———. 1989. "Cutting Deficit Is Political Loser Even for Soviets." *The Wall Street Journal.* April 17.

Berliner, Joseph S. 1976. *The Innovation Decision in Soviet Industry.* Cambridge: MIT Press.

Bhagwati, Jagdish N. 1982. "Directly Unproductive, Profit-Seeking (DUP) Activities." *Journal of Political Economy* 90 (October): 988–1002.

Bulgakov, Mikhail. 1967. *The Master and Margarita.* New York: New American Library. English translation copyright by Harvill Press and Harper & Row, Publishers, Inc., 1967.

Burlatsky, Fedor. 1988. "Khrushchev: Shtrikhi k politicheskomu portreti." *Literaturnaia gazeta* 8 (February 24): 14.

Butler, William E. 1988. "Legal Reform in the Soviet Union." The Harriman Institute *Forum* 1 (September): 1–8.

Central Intelligence Agency. 1987. *Handbook of Economic Statistics.* Washington, D.C.

———. 1988. *Sharply Higher Budget Deficits Threaten Perestroyka.* Directorate of Intelligence, SOV 88-10043. Washington, D.C.

———. 1989. *USSR: Estimates of Personal Income and Savings.* Directorate of Intelligence, SOV 89-10035. Washington, D.C.

Desai, Padma. 1987. *The Soviet Economy: Problems and Prospects.* Oxford: Basil Blackwell.

———. 1989. "Perestroika, Prices, and the Ruble Problem." The Harriman Institute *Forum* 11 (November): 1–8.

Desai, Padma, and Ricardo Martin. 1983. "Efficiency Loss from Resource Misallocation in Soviet Industry." *Quarterly Journal of Economics* 97 (September): 442–56.

Ericson, Richard E. 1988. "The New Enterprise Law." The Harriman Institute *Forum* 1 (February): 1–8.

Gorbachev, Mikhail. 1987. *Perestroika: New Thinking for Our Country and the World*. New York: Harper and Row.

Gregory, Paul R., and Robert C. Stuart. 1981. *Soviet Economic Structure and Performance*. New York: Harper and Row.

Gurevich, Alan. 1987. "Joint Ventures with the West: Recent Developments." *Radio Liberty Research*. RL 263/87 (July 5).

Hanson, Philip. 1981. *Trade and Technology in Soviet-Western Relations*. New York: Columbia University Press.

Hewett, Ed A. 1988a. *Reforming the Soviet Economy*. Washington, D.C.: The Brookings Institution.

———. 1988b. "The Foreign Economic Factor in *Perestroika*." The Harriman Institute *Forum* 1 (August): 1–8.

Holzman, Franklyn D. 1976. *International Trade Under Communism: Politics and Economics*. New York: Basic Books.

Irwin, Douglas A. 1989. "Political Economy and Peel's Repeal of the Corn Laws." *Economics and Politics* 1, 1 (Spring): 41–60.

Joint Economic Committee (JEC). 1988. U.S. Congress. *Gorbachev's Economic Plans*. Vols. 1 and 2. Washington, D.C.

Kennan, George. 1947. "The Sources of Soviet Conduct." *Foreign Affairs* 25 (July): 566–82.

Kornai, Janos. 1980. *Economics of Shortage*. Amsterdam: North-Holland Company.

Lakshin, Vladimir. 1980. *Solzhenitsyn, Tvardovsky, and Novy Mir*. Cambridge: MIT Press.

Lerner, Eugene M. 1956. "Inflation in the Confederacy, 1861–65." In *Studies in the Quantity Theory of Money*, edited by Milton Freedman, 163–75. Chicago: University of Chicago Press.

McIntyre, Joan F. 1988a. "The U.S.S.R's Hard Currency Trade and Payments Position," 474–88. In Joint Economic Committee, U.S. Congress, *Gorbachev's Economic Plans*, vol. 2. Washington, D.C.

———. 1988b. "Soviet Efforts to Revamp the Foreign Trade Sector," 489–503. In Joint Economic Committee, U.S. Congress, *Gorbachev's Economic Plans*, vol. 2. Washington, D.C.

Medvedev, Roy. 1983. *Khrushchev: A Biography*. Garden City, N.Y.: Anchor Press/Doubleday.

Nove, Alec. 1977. *The Soviet Economic System*. London: George Allen and Unwin.

Pickersgill, Joyce. 1976. "Soviet Household Saving Behavior." *The Review of Economics and Statistics* 58 (May): 139–47.

Rumer, Boris. 1990. " 'Abalkanization' of Soviet Reform." *Problems of Communism* (January–February): 74–82.

Schroeder, Gertrude E. 1987. "Anatomy of Gorbachev's Economic Reform." *Soviet Economy* 3 (July–September): 219–41.

Sestanovich, Stephen. 1990. "Gorbachev's Last Summit?" *The New York Times*. May 31.

Shipler, David K. 1983. *Russia: Broken Idols, Solemn Dreams.* New York: New York Times Book Co.

Thornton, Judith. 1971. "Differential Capital Charges and Resource Allocation in Soviet Industry." *Journal of Political Economy* 79: 545–61.

Tsentral'noe Statisticheskoe Upravlenie pri Sovete Ministrov SSSR. Various numbers. *Narodnoe Khoziaistvo SSSR (Narkhoz).* Moscow.

U.S. Congress. 1989. *The Soviet Economy in 1988: Gorbachev Changes Course.* A report by the Central Intelligence Agency and the Defense Intelligence Agency presented to the Subcommittee on National Security Economics of the Joint Economic Committee. Washington, D.C.

————. 1990. *The Soviet Economy Stumbles Badly in 1989.* A report presented by the Central Intelligence Agency and the Defense Intelligence Agency to the Technology and National and Security Subcommittee of the Joint Economic Committee. Washington, D.C.

U.S. Department of Agriculture. 1989a. *CPE Agriculture Report* 2, 1 (January–February). Washington, D.C.

————. 1989b. *USSR: Agriculture and Trade Report.* RS-89-1. Washington, D.C.

————. 1990. *USSR: Agriculture and Trade Report.* RS-90-1. Washington, D.C.

U.S. Department of Commerce. 1985. *Financing of Research, Development, and Innovation in the USSR.* Foreign Economic Report no. 22. Washington, D.C.: Bureau of the Census.

Weitzman, Martin L. 1986. *The Share Economy.* Cambridge: Harvard University Press.

Index

Abalkin, Leonid, 47, 67, 148n, 184, 186, 191
Abkhazia, 126, 144
Academy of Pedagogical Sciences, 79
Academy of Sciences, 44
acceleration, 48, 87, 168
accountants, 18
adjustment problems, 95, 101
administered direction, 10
administrative efficiency, 14
Afanasyev, Viktor, 76
Afghanistan, 83, 85, 86, 88, 95
Aganbegyan, Abel, 44, 47, 49, 56, 166, 205n.2, 206n.3, 207n.9
agriculture: Brezhnev reforms in, 44; in China, 36, 105; current reforms in, 57–58, 104, 108, 150–55, 161; in Hungary, 36, 105; importance to reforms, 105–6, 146; Khrushchev and, 49; management of, 31; problems of, 15–19; Stalin and, 48–49; taxation, 35, 155, 192; Third World, 88
Aitmatov, Chingiz, 61
alcoholism, 28
Alexander I, Czar, 140
Alexander II, Czar, 140
alienation, 6, 31, 46, 79
allocation, 11, 14, 21, 45, 205n.2
AlphaGraphics Printshops of the Future, 159
American Trade Consortium, 160
Andreeva, Nina, 64, 74
Angola, 88, 89, 95
annual plans, 42
Anti-ballistic Missile (ABM) Treaty, 93

antisemitism, 120
apathy, 79
Aral Sea, 136
Arbatov, Georgii, 76, 86–87, 95
Archer-Daniels-Midland Co., 160
Armenia and Armenians, 69, 70, 111, 120, 128, 140, 143, 145, 200
arms control, 7, 83, 92–96, 98, 109, 138
arms sales, 89
associations, 45
auctions, 161, 182
autonomy, political, 69, 70, 140
autonomy of enterprises, 27, 28, 32, 33–34, 46, 66
Azerbaijan and Azerbaijanis, 69, 70, 111, 120, 126, 128, 140, 143–45, 200

Baku, 145
Baltic republics, 69, 70, 76, 120, 122, 127–28, 130–31, 136–40, 142, 145
bankruptcies, 13
banks and banking, 27, 32, 39, 40, 164, 165, 173, 176, 184–86
Belorussia, 124, 127, 131, 136, 143, 144
Bergson, Abram, 205n.1
Berliner, Joseph, 14
Bhagwati, Jagdish, 118
birth rate, 129
blat, 6
Bogomolov, Oleg, 85
bonds, 164, 176
bonuses, 10, 11, 12, 17, 18, 45; export bonus, 23
Bovin, Aleksandr, 85, 86
Brest Peace, The, 74–75